Security for the Pope
In a Violent and Rebellious World

Jordan Nyenyembe

Langaa Research & Publishing CIG
Mankon, Bamenda

Publisher
Langaa RPCIG
Langaa Research & Publishing Common Initiative Group
P.O. Box 902 Mankon
Bamenda
North West Region
Cameroon
Langaagrp@gmail.com
www.langaa-rpcig.net

Distributed in and outside N. America by African Books Collective
orders@africanbookscollective.com
www.africanbookcollective.com

ISBN: 9956-728-87-X

© Jordan Nyenyembe 2012

DISCLAIMER
All views expressed in this publication are those of the author and do not necessarily reflect the views of Langaa RPCIG.

Dedication

To the Late Rev. Father John K. Nchimbi "Socrates"

A Brother and Friend

Table of Contents

Acknowledgements... v

Introduction.. vii

1. Are You Afraid of an Assassination Attempt?................1
Relevant Question at a right Time.. 1
The "Yes" and "No" of the Pope... 11
Testimony of Christian Courage... 14

2. In the Shoes of the Fisherman................................. 19
Galilean Man designated as "Rock".. 21
Peter's Sword and the Mind of Jesus...................................... 25
Prisoner in Maximum Security Jail... 29
Flight from Persecutions: But Quo Vadis?.............................. 32
Model of a Genuine Disciple... 34

3. Targeting Popes..41
Mehmet Ali Agca: Skilled Shooter who missed Target.............. 41
Rebellious Priest who was Intercepted.................................... 44
Susanna Maiolo's leap in St. Peter's Basilica........................... 45
What can we learn from those Attacks?..................................47

4. Like a Lamb led to Slaughter...................................61
Cross Bearer who is not Crusader.. 62
The Pallium shouldered Pontiff across Boarders...................... 72

5. Universal Pastor in Pope Mobile............................. 77
Sheltering the Pope for Security... 77
In Need of the Pope for Security.. 80

6. Head of State Not like Others..................................... 87
The Pope and His Cabinet.. 87
Audiences from the Window..92
The Vatican Flag- An Emblem of Peace.............................. 97
A pastor not Commander in Chief.. 99

7. Global Youth Shockwaves.. 109
Global Protests: Rebellion from Below................................. 115
The Pope: Father and Friend of Young People....................... 119

8. Moral Pitfall of Nation States.................................... 127
The Human Heart is at Stake... 130
The Papacy without Tiara.. 133
The Vatican State: Dismissing Wrong Assumptions............... 135
The Vatican is not a Nation – State.................................... 138
The Vatican is not an Autocratic State................................145
The Vatican State: Chair of Charity and Truth..................... 149

Concluding Reflections... 159

Selected Bibliography.. 167

Index..173

Acknowledgements

Writing a book for an adult audience and which treats a serious issue like security is an endeavour not without tension. In the first place tension develops as to where one is to find appropriate and adequate sources. Ideas about rebellion and violence which form the sub-title of the book may look threatening and awful, and therefore, in the second place a tension results from doubt as to whether an author can find interested persons who could proof- read the project at hand. What follows, then, is an imperfect attempt to thank all those who offered me a helping hand to overcome such tensions.

At the earliest stage the draft was shared to some of my friends in Vienna (Austria), which was my temporal home during my studies there. I entrusted the work to Andrea Ambrozy, Paschal Mfilinge, Fathers Michael Mwambegu, Edward Mwale and Samuel Kiprugut. The first draft of the work appeared in its humble form, yet all these friends offered a fundamental support for me to forge ahead. Words of encouragement from them motivated me to keep writing the book.

At a later stage, with the aid of electronic mail I passed the manuscript to a distant place. I sought help from Fr. Bruno Mgaya, and through him to benefit the proof reading of Sharon L. Michel. A gifted reader such as Sharon is; placed the work under her judicious corrections. Sharon wielded her sharp grammatical skills to expose critical gaps and flaws in some sentences. I appreciate the time and diligence she gave to the manuscript.

Finally, I have to thank the Editorial Board at Langaa for the interest with the work and for offering to publish it. I have dedicated the book to the late Rev. Fr. John Kornel Nchimbi an outstanding teacher, a gifted thinker, and philosopher. His death by car accident, June 2012 came untimely, and it happened at the moment when the Publisher was looking at the proposal of this manuscript.

Introduction

The window of the papal apartment is a focal point of international media all the time the Pope has an audience with pilgrims, particularly when he speaks on issues of global significance. One of such thrilling moments is at the occasion when he preaches and prays for peace in the world. Usually a dove is let go from the window to commemorate the event. At different occasions doves have been released by the Pope only to return back to him. On 30 January 2005, three months before his death, Pope John Paul II was flanked by two children who released two doves. One of the doves seemed reluctant to fly away from the Pope. It returned and landed on his left shoulder, after which he released it for the second time.

Following the practice of his predecessors, Pope Benedict XVI at two different occasions, and in order to mark the World Day of Peace released a dove which came back intending to remain in the palace. It seems likely that the doves at all these occasions were gripped by fear of the violent world in front of them. Thus one may presume that the doves were prompted to return to a more serene and peaceful atmosphere of the papal apartment. Such incidents remind us of what happened at the time of Noah. The surface of the earth had been flooded with heavy down pours for forty days, on daylights and in the nights. Noah and his family were protected in the Ark which was built by God's instruction. After all these days he sent a dove in order to know if violent flooding waters had subsided. When the dove came back Noah knew that chaos and turbulence have not yet gone down (see Gen. 8:6-12). But unlike the time of Noah, doves released by the popes have not come back bearing on their beaks fleshly plucked olive leaves to usher a prospectus for peace in contemporary world.

The above reflections strongly came as I was writing this book. Two events dominated the coverage of international and local media, precisely at the time I was developing the manuscript of this book. The first one concerns Anders Behring Breivik, a Norwegian man in his early thirties years reported on 22 July 2011. This man planted a bomb in the government buildings in Oslo and then rushed to the camping Island of Utoya to shoot innocent students who were spending time together during their annual camp-out. There were over 80 people killed in both instances.

The second event occurred at the beginning of August, 2011 in London (UK), where groups of young people stormed the streets in a wave of violence, looting and setting fire to buildings and police cars throughout the city. This drama spread to other cities like Birmingham, Liverpool and Manchester. The youth in hooded shirts fought running battles with police, smashing windows and setting fire to clothing shops! These incidents and many others of the like reflect a volatile situation of recurring violence in the world we live today.

Why Write a Book about the Security of the Pope?

Looking at events as they are reported globally, violence takes place constantly. Perpetrators lack a complete sense or have little sense about the sacredness of human life, and have no respect for places of worship. In our days we are constantly informed of shootings taking place in church buildings during worship services and some directly pointed at ministers themselves. Incidents of dismissal killings and murder are on daily basis.

The theme of "security" is one of the compelling agendas in international conferences and workshops today. "Security" is a new theme in academic circles. The international community had just begun to be interested with the themes of peace and security after the cold war ended. This was so because, for a long time, the violence that affected the Majority World (Third World Countries) was considered to be a development problem and not a security one. Meanwhile, powerful nations with strong military capacities 'turned their attention from deterrence and inter-bloc rivalries to a wide range of new security agendas, including the peace building development nexus in fragile or post conflict states' (Watson 2011:9).

It is just recently that the security debate has taken a new focus towards the recognition of the concept of "human security" as a counter - balance to a mere state - and/or regime security. The novelty of this focus is to place the individual at the centre of security and emphasizes not only freedom from threat, but also the need for economic, social and political security of the human person. In this view point, security is now ranked in a hierarchy of public good as the central precondition for political and social order.

At no other time of history has media frenzy been fuelling attacks of hate against the Pope, Church ministers and the Catholic Church itself as it is now. In 2010 journalist Bob Ellis, wrote a piece of article for *ABC Australia* that was calling for bombing the Vatican, unusual in its tone and yet revealing anti-Catholicism trend. This is what a part of his article reads:

...Why then do we not bomb the Vatican and obliterate Italy for harbouring this criminal (the Pope) mastermind, this known protector of evil predators? Why we do not pursue him through the sewers of Europe and riddle his corpse with bullets? Why are we not bombing the Vatican (Corren 2012:21).

The idea of the journalist above may be dismissed as mere manifestation of a bizarre journalism that should not receive attention. To our estimate, this is not an issue which has to be ignored. It should be construed in the context of systematic violence as organized by some state security agents in the name of national security on the one hand, and terrorist networks in order to express their grievances on the other. Both the state agents and terrorists do sort out individuals to be eliminated. In several occasions they make known their intention to pursue their "enemies" but in most cases the hunting remains secrete. Such a situation has paved a way for the security field to employ concepts such as: "targeted killings" and "targeted selection."

The explicit selection of the Vatican and the mention of the person of the Pope from the extract above have to be considered within the framework of "targeted killings" and "targeted selection" which is embedded into the social, political and cultural dynamics of society. A global terrorist franchise, for example, exhibits certain characteristics namely: the release of video messages, and attacks on symbolic targets such as church buildings, and its personnel among others. Therefore, the selection of Vatican City by the journalist, the author of the article partly quoted above reflects the change of discourse in political violence. Sacred places and consecrated persons are no longer "outside the lists" of organized violence.

This situation invites every concerned Catholic to take matters of security seriously than we have treated it so far. The protection of the person of the Holy Father cannot be left in the hands of security personnel alone. To say it in other words, the issue of Pope's security cannot be separated from the welfare of global Catholic community. What we recognize today from what passes on in the media and in secular discourses about the Roman Catholic Church is alerting. The Church is a persecuted institution. Some articles posted in the internet carry words of hate against the Church. One of the article posted in the internet on the 2 June 2012, describes the Roman Catholic Church as an unwanted institution. The title of the article run as follows: 'the Catholic Church is Dangerous, Outdated, and should Dissolve' (Riggio 2012). Michael Coren a Jew and a converted Catholic provides a telling testimony about his own experience as to how he was treated as member of Jewish Religion and now as devoted Catholic. 'Being part Jewish, on the other hand, has positively helped me in my career, whereas my serious Catholicism has led to at least two firings and my doors in media being closed. So while anti-Semitism is vile and constant, being an observant Catholic, at least in the Western world, can lead to other different but equally difficult problems' (Corren 2011:5-6).

A treatise on Church's security is an urgent one. While undertaking this project as a pioneer, we recognize that it is an adventure for someone who is neither an expert in the affairs of the Holy See and the Vatican State, nor has specialized formation in international relations. Taking this fact into consideration, we think it is appropriate to inform our readers that this book is written from a pastoral point of view and by a pastoral theologian. Although it is etched in and supported with library research it is not tailored to provide an academic screw about security and peace; rather it seeks to provide a spiritual reflection surrounding the issue of security. It is woven together to serve pastoral and spiritual purposes. While it intends to enlighten the mind, it targets to reach the heart of the human person which ever yearn to be warmed a fresh. This book is simultaneously a modest and an ambitious daring. It is modest in the sense that it delves into the theme of security from a theological point of view which the author is conversant, but also daring because it opens a new debate, and ventures a novel field. This book is written to stimulate reflections and provide a food of thought to digest.

Following the attempts on the life of Blessed Pope John Paul II in 1983, and the aggression Pope Benedict XVI endured in St. Peter's Basilica in 2009, what has come out for the public to read mostly were accounts of reporters and journalists, some accusing the security personnel, some simply narrating the event as they have happened. We have seldom read the reaction of theologians on these events. Moreover, existing literature on peace and discourses that surrounds it tend to blame governments on how they have failed to ensure the security of its population in cases of attack. Such literature conveys the idea that more military resources are needed to defeat enemies. It appeals for intensified strategic action geared at curbing the shortage of armed protection. Events happening in the contemporary era, amplifies the situation of insecurity which necessitates a reflection about the security of the Pope as well.

The New Age of Martyrdom

Today we are experiencing global warming, global displacement of masses of people, and the breakdown of traditional institutions. Many people feel insecure as traditional institutions which once guaranteed security are disintegrating. Intense poverty and sufferings have robbed many of them a hope in the future. In situations such as these, inevitably what ensues is the emergence of "pseudo fortune tellers" who claim to have been empowered through heavenly vision to pronounce deliverance to humankind. The daily grip of fear, uncertainty, and neglect paves a way to the development of a 'culture of cataclysmic doom in which "false prophets" speculate in wild and bizarre ways about the dark and dangerous future that likely will befall us all' (O' Murchu 2008:208). These prophets of doom preach about the immanent end of the world and calls people to renounce everything including life. The trends enveloping have resulted into popular religiosity which has heightened fantasies for martyrdom as manner of embracing the end of time.

It is in this atmosphere we see a resurging wave of suicide bombers. They are a result of an indoctrination that acts of self immolation contribute to accessing a better life in the next world denied here on earth due to injustices. For a suicide bomber the act of "martyrdom" is a guarantee for procuring high reward in heaven. Some radical Islamic groups circumvent suicidal aspect of human bombing by euphemistic labelling: instead of calling their operations as "suicide bombings," they conceptualize it as "martyrdom works." Those young people who are ready to volunteer to die as martyrs are hailed for offering to die a heroic death. Pioneers of the suicide bombings create posters, websites, and public exhibit to honour their "martyrs" and publicize their "heroic" sacrifice. As for those who terminate their lives as suicide bombers, they are lauded through rituals and ceremonies. Words of praise and practices which are focused towards those who commit attacks on specific targets idealize the act of martyrdom and elevate its underlying significance. The rituals and ceremonies accorded to suicide bombers extol such acts of extreme violence. Such gestures honours the cruel terror committed while neglecting the death of innocents such attacks inflicts. The idea that one can commit suicide under the umbrella of *Jihad* and in the name of *Allah* upsets the image of religion as a vehicle for peace. Muslims are rallied with the idea to recapture the spirit of resistance against the *kaffirs*, the non believers who must be eliminated if they do not want to convert into Islam. According to some extremists, Islam must be spread everywhere in the world, and infidels have to be defeated. One way to achieve this goal is to be ready to die martyrs for Islam. What is at stake is not the right of Muslims to preach their religion, but the radical idea that everywhere efforts must be done to create Islamic states, and to pressurize all non Muslim citizens to follow Islamic laws; the *sharia*. The 2007 Interreligious Conference which took place in Abuja Nigeria is enlightening to the point we make here. The conference brought together Nigerian outstanding Christian and Muslim clerics. Archbishop John Onaiyekan, the Archbishop of Abuja took part in dialogue with leadership of the National Mosque in the city. One of the Muslim leaders argued that Christians should not feel threatened by *Shari'a* because they too would have rights in *Shari'a* courts. The Archbishop rejected the proposal, 'that's not a right we want it is not a right we accept' (Allen Jr 2009:63).

Increasingly, extreme forms of Islam encourage and promote martyrdom. 'The whole issue of the intentions behind the willingness of the martyr to die for what he or she believes has become a burning subject in contemporary life because of the almost weekly accounts we have in the press about Islamic suicide bombers, who immolate themselves as part of the *Jihad* against the perceived enemies of Islam' (Cunningham 2011:15). There is a trend by some Muslim clerics to fuel the idea that Islam is discriminated against and marginalized in the world. This trend encourages *Jihad* as the way to exhibit the grievances. Suicide bombers are hailed as heroes, and declared outright as martyrs. The Pope as a peace maker who rejects violence as a way to spread the faith, risks angering some Muslims and can find himself a target of radical sections of Islam.

Pondering on what is actually taking place in those places where Christians are a minority, the Vatican has thought it relevant to put forward to the international community the proposal to establish an international day against the worldwide persecution of Christians. Archbishop Dominique Mamberti, the Vatican's Secretary of Relations with states, announced the need for an international day on Dec. 6, 2011 at the Organization for Security and Cooperation in Europe's Ministerial Council gathered in the Lithuanian capital of Vilnius (see Kerr 2011:2). According to the Archbishop, the celebration of a day against the discrimination of Christians; 'might prove to be an important sign that governments are willing to deal with this serious issue' (Kerr 2011:2). During his message for the World Day of Peace in 2011, Pope Benedict XVI expressed openly that "many Christians experience daily affronts and often live in fear because of their pursuit of truth, their faith in Jesus Christ and their heartfelt plea for respect for religious freedom." The Pope made it clear that the situation as it is today posed a 'threat to security and peace' (Benedict XVI 2011).

In defending the rights of both Christians and Muslims to practice their religion in the public sphere the Pope risks to irritate some Christian fundamentalists. It should be made clear that, extreme elements of Christianity poses danger to world peace as well. In addition, to answer the violence inflicted on the Christians by radical Muslims, some Christians regard the use of force as necessary to defend Jesus Christ and his Church. On January 19, 1999, for example, riots broke out between Christians and Muslims in Ambon City, the capital of the Maluku Islands in Indonesia that would last for more than three years, leaving almost dozens of thousands of people dead. Abé, a Christian bodyguard in Ambon fought Muslims during the riots. When a journalist asked him why he was fighting, he answered: 'we fight for Christ, not for ourselves' (Van Liere 2011:329). There is always a danger for Christians while facing threat to their lives in justifying violence as defending Christ and the Church. Moreover, within Christianity, there are some ecclesial communities which spearhead aggressive evangelism with the intension to proselytise Muslims and Christians from mainline churches. This spirit rather encourages a vicious circle of violence. Meanwhile the Pope in his fidelity to speak the will of God to all the people is a potential "enemy" to Christians and Muslims with extreme views and those who opts for violence.

Given the circumstances of terror and aggressive behaviour such as we have today the theme of the "Security for the Pope" is relevant. The Bishop of Rome faces death every single day. It is either from what he preaches leading him oftentimes to be hated in view of his faith witness; notably the *odium fidei*, or from what he does in practicing charity. He may be hunted down for witness of charity namely the *odium caritatis*.

An Era of Protests and Demonstrations

The media reports repeatedly about demonstrations and protests taking place in different parts of the globe. From Brazil to Australia, Greece to Egypt, indeed in many places, hundreds of thousands of people have taken to the streets to demand social change as well as economic reform. On 13 February, 2003 following the huge demonstration of over fourteen million people in over 240 cities in the world against the impending U.S war on Iraq with the aim to topple the regime, the *New York Times* reported that, there are now two global powers- the American empire and global protestors for peace. It is impossible nowadays to overlook the political, social and economic impacts brought by these demonstrations and protests.

Papal visits in some parts of Europe have been greeted by demonstrators and protestors. Shortly before Pope Benedict XVI's visit to United Kingdom on Sept, 16-19, 2010, there were some voices from among academicians and authors led by prominent atheists Richard Dawkins and Christopher Hitchens who mobilized the people by signing a public letter calling for the Pope to be arrested. They reiterated that the Pope should not be given state visit. The pair solicited the accusations that the Holy Fathers had committed crimes against humanity for his alleged cover-up of intimate abuse in the Catholic Church. According to them the Pope had delayed the punishment for a paedophile priest in the US for the "good of the Universal Church" while still as cardinal. Those who wanted the Pope arrested had planned to send their accusations to English courts and some sought to consult the International Criminal court. In their insistence they rejected the idea that the Holy See is a state and that the Pope is not the head of state. The Holy See however, insisted that the Pope is a head of the state and has the same legal status of immunity as all heads of state have.

Things were not different during the Pope's visit to Spain for the World Youth Day in September 2011. Shortly before the visit there, thousands of protesters marched in Madrid opposing the visit due to financial constraints which the country was undergoing. As protestors and demonstrators marched in Madrid, clashes with

Spanish police were reported which caused some of the protestors to get arrested and injured. The situation of confrontation and protest which occur during the papal visits raise the anxiety as regard the security of the Bishop of Rome.

The title of the Book

The main title of the book is "Security for the Pope." The preposition "'for' connects two nouns: "security" and the "Pope." Security can simply be defined as state of living without fear. The word "Pope" means "Father" it is used in the Roman Catholic Church for the Holy Father. "Security for the Pope" speaks of all the provisions which are to be in place to ensure that the life of the Holy Father is secured. The book does not use the preposition "of" the Pope to avoid the idea that the security of the Holy Father is apart from the security of the Church. Speaking of the "Security for the Pope" conveys an idea of the close connection between his security and that of all members of the Church. It invites every Catholic faithful to be responsible for the protection of the Holy Father. The Church has not emerged from its own power. It is born and sustained by the power of the Holy Spirit. "Security for the Pope" is a title seeking to unleash the message that the security of the Pope's life depends on divine support as well. Therefore this title underlines Church's dependency on God's protection.

Now to the sub-title: "In a Violent and Rebellious World." Violence means existence of disorder involving bloody conflicts, massacres and injuries inflicted on people. Rebellion means the attitude of disobedience to authorities and disloyalty. In the Bible the word "rebellion" is used to express a state of disobedience of the Israelites against the will of God. It refers to the attitude of not wanting to fulfil what God commands. The concept is used to express the hard-necked attitude of the people, "Ah Lord, great and awesome God, we have sinned and done wrong, acted wickedly and rebelled" (Dan 9:5). Again while praising God as merciful, Prophet Daniel underlines the rebellious attitude of human beings, "To the Lord our God belong mercy and forgiveness for we have rebelled against him, and have not obeyed the voice of the LORD our God" (Dan 9:9-10). Thus the Israelites were told in the past, "Today, if you hear his voice, do not harden your hearts as in the rebellion" (Hebr. 3:8, 15;).

Rebellion against authority is widely spread today. In many occasion people are at odds even with those laws and orders legally enacted by ecclesiastical and secular authorities. In politics, in business, as well as in church affairs, mistrust between those in position of authority and their subjects is evident. World religions have failed to provide ethical and moral models in different areas. There is crisis within religions. This unrest in religious institutions paves a way to polarizing tendencies between conservatives and liberals, traditionalists and modernists and even Catholic theologians are divided between the communion scholars (those whose theology seeks to maintain unity and loyalty to the Pope) and the Kingdom of God scholars (those whose theology wrestle on issues of justice, ecology, ecumenism etc). The grand narratives are criticized and considered unfit to address new questions and anxieties. Posters and protests are also held in churches as tensions mounts. Some people enter their signatories to highlight their rejection of some decisions made by church leaders. Pressure groups and rebellious movements they organize, bring unrest and the feeling of insecurity among leaders and those under them.

Archbishop Malcolm Ranjith, the Sri Lankan Secretary of the Congregation for Divine Worship, is perhaps the first highest ranking Catholic official to shift the use of language by employing the word "rebellion" to describe disloyalty against authorities, instead of regular terms such as *dissenters* (those differing with authorities on doctrinal positions) and *reformers* (persons differing with the hierarchy on practical matters). Now the word *rebellion* is used to express the spirit of the time, where disloyalty is always accompanied with some form of violence. In an interview with Bruno Volpe, the Archbishop was asked: "Your Excellency, what kind of reception has Benedict XVI's *Motu Proprio* which allows priests to celebrate the Holy Masses in the Tridentine rite had?" He answered:

There have been positive reactions and, it's pointless to deny it, criticism and opposing positions, also on the part of theologians, liturgists, priests, bishops, and even cardinals. Frankly, I don't understand this distancing from and, let's just say it, *rebellion* against the Pope. I invite all, above, all shepherds, to obey the Pope, who is the successor of Peter. Bishops, in particular, swore loyalty to the Pontiff...You know that there have been, on the part of some dioceses, even interpretive documents which inexplicably aim at putting limits on the Pope's *Motu Proprio*. Behind these actions there are hidden, on the other hand, prejudices of an ideological kind and, on the other hand, pride, one of the gravest sins (Lash 2008:260,261).

Disloyalty to authority threatens the welfare of the Holy Father and those who assist him to carry his ministry. Now it has gone beyond doctrinal and moral matters. It escalates to water down ethical codes of conduct in places of administration. The leakage of confidential documents of the Pope and the Holy See to the public as discovered recently is a disgusting revelation. The so called *Vatileaks* manifests in its own way the situation of insecurity the Church faces at our time.

The Summary of the Chapters

The first chapter of this book takes seriously the question "Are you Afraid of an Assassination Attempt?" which the German journalist Peter Seewald posed to the Pope. The question sheds light to the concern for the security of the leader of the Catholic Church. The possibility of an assassination plot against the Pope in this violent and rebellious world cannot be dismissed. The answer the Pope gives to the question provide a catechetical illumination for all Christians.

Chapter two tries to inform the reader about the circumstances of insecurity which St. Peter, the fisherman from Galilee faced. This is necessarily so because all the popes who followed him are regarded as "Successors of Peter." The chapter looks at the life of St. Peter and the difficulties he endured. The profile of his insecurity offers spiritual insights regarding the idea of papal security.

After learning the life of St. Peter and his death as martyr despite the effort to flee from the persecutions in Rome, we move to peruse the fate which contemporary popes have faced. This is done in chapter three. In this chapter information is provided about the assassination attempts on the life of Pope John Paul II (1983) and the physical aggression on Pope Benedict (2009). Reading how these attacks happened and learning how their lives were spared may provide spiritual wisdom.

Chapter four presents the person of the Pope as a cross bearer and a pallium carrier around the world. The chapter looks at the Pope as a universal pastor who brings the image of Jesus Christ the good shepherd to the whole world.

Chapter five looks at the Pope as a pastor who provides assurance to his distressed flock. The hunger for spirituality by many Christians today shows how frequently Catholics all over the world want the assurance through the presence of their local pastors and the global pastor.

Chapter six treats the Pope as head of state. It tries to inform the reader about what kind of head of State the Pope is in relationship to other heads of nation- states. The survey on his cabinet, which is composed of cardinal prefects who heads the Roman curia helps to show why cardinals, who assist the Pope to govern the universal Church, are a witness to the faith that is animated by the power of the crucified Christ. The chapter concludes by stating that the Pope is the head of state not a commander in chief.

Chapter seven probes the rebellion of the youth around the world. It begins with riots and youth violence in France in 2005, and then moves to the Tunisian and Egyptian revolutions as well. The anger of young people is directed to governments and to the head of states. This makes a basis for the fresh look at the relationship the Pope has with the Catholic young people around the world. The chapter ponders also the advent of protests and demonstrations, some of which are violent. In its final part, this chapter appreciates the pastoral wisdom of the Church to engage young people. In this way young people feel that indeed they are in communion and are the Church themselves.

The last chapter tries to underscore the fact that the Vatican state in general and the Holy See in particular have a long history. The Church has legitimacy for its autonomous statehood's separate from that of nation-states. The chapter reiterates that cooperation between the two separate powers is necessary.

1

Are you afraid of an Assassination attempt?

During his conversation with Peter Seewald recorded in the book *Light of the World: the Pope, the Church, and the Signs of the Time*; Pope Benedict XVI is asked a total of 222 questions which are divided into three parts: each part made up of six chapters. The first part is entitled "Signs of the Time." The second part has as its title, "the Pontificate," and the third, bears the title of "Where do we go from here?" Of all the 222 questions an arresting one concerns the Pope's personal security. The question is formulated in this way; "Are you afraid of an assassination attempt?" from which the Pope offers a straight answer, "No." We shall look in detail about this response at the last section of this chapter.

Relevant Question at a right Time

In a world dominated by fear and terror threats the question "are you afraid of an assassination attempt?" comes just at the right time. Peter Seewald an award winning journalist had previously had two interviews with Joseph Ratzinger, when he was Cardinal Prefect of the Congregation of Faith. In all the previous interviews the question about the security of the then cardinal never appeared. The Journalist does not raise the question about the security of the cardinal but asking it when the same person is now Bishop of Rome merits an analytical assessment.

The Pope is not a Superman

The analysis of the question is crucial especially in today's Western culture. Many people are afraid of anything about death and the dead. The Pope answering "No" to the question if he is afraid of the assassination attempt may seem superficial for some; and as a correct answer deserving a "superman" to the others. An accomplished person such as the Pope is; is regarded by some people as *Übermensch* a superman. The answer of the Pope may just consolidate the false idea some people have about him. To most of them, a superman should not have to fear death. In Western culture many people are based on the illusion of invulnerability. A good number of people fail to grasp the human vulnerability; indeed all members of human family are vulnerable.

A true story is narrated about Mohammad Ali, former world heavyweight champion. During one of his trips he boarded a plane to a designated destination where he was scheduled for a fight to defend his title. On this trip the captain of the plane abruptly announced, "Approaching severe turbulence. Would passengers and crew fasten seatbelts immediately?" The crew hurried up down the aisles to check that everyone had fixed the belt accordingly. One flight stewardess noticed Mohammad Ali toward the front of the aircraft relaxed and his seatbelt undone. "Excuse me, sir. Would you please fasten your seatbelt?" She asked. "The captain has advised this could be quite rough." The champion boxer looked at the lady and confidently retorted "Supermen don't need seatbelt." The plane attendant shot back directly to him "supermen don't need plane!" Such a false and seemingly show off pretention of the boxer of harbouring "fear proof" to impending life threat is not true in so far as our human experience is concerned. The Pope is not a superman, like every Jesus' disciples he is called to holiness, and 'saints are...not superhuman or angelic but fully human, as alive as God intended them to be' (Barron 2011:196).

The question "are you afraid of an assassination attempt?" is squarely addressed to the person who holds the post as the Vicar of Christ in the world. It is crafted correctly. The choice of the word "assassination" is more appropriate to converse the idea the journalist wants to underline to all his readers. This is truly so due to the fact that: 'When a killing is labelled an assassination, the act, actors and associated effects are imbued with a level of importance and status that is often absent in other forms of political violence or killing' (Gayson 2012:26). The question is not put like "Are you Afraid of Death?" It would take an angel who is not mortal not to be afraid of death because angels being immortal do not have the experience of death. As a devoted Christian, Peter Seewald knows that death is a must and natural for every created being. Assassination, however, is death inflicted on someone by another human person causing unnatural disruption of one's life.

As mortals we are afraid of death, since it is associated with a loss of physical organism. The process of dying not least of times involve sufferings and in most cases severe pains. In addition, death separates us from those whom we love and know. It is a sad experience. According to Pope Benedict, 'death is loneliness *par excellence*' (Benedict XVI 2003). It would be an absurdity to ask the Pope if he is afraid of death. Jesus Christ as a human person was afraid of death. While at Gethsemane with Peter, Johannes and Jacob were aware that the Roman and Jewish authorities were sending soldiers to arrest him. He said to them, "I am deeply grieved, even to death; remain here, and keep awake. And going a little farther, he threw himself on the ground and prayed that, if it were possible, the hour might pass from him" (Mt 26:36-46; Mk 14:32-36; Lk 22:39-46). One of the qualities of brave people is to admit their weakness and even their fears. Once the Archbishop Oscar Romero was sitting on a beach with a friend, and he asked his friend whether he was afraid to die. The friend replied that he was not, and Romero said, 'But I am. I am afraid to die; and yet he gave his life' (Radcliffe 2005:72).

Not all fear is negative. Indeed, fear serves life. Think about the positive effect of adrenaline that energizing one to flee from an advancing crocodile at river side. The Bible wants us, however, to discern what kind of fear are we subjected to. The phrase "be not afraid" appears now and then in Holy Scripture. It refers to one's reaction to positive or negative manifestation of power, often of divine epiphany. The disciple's reaction to Jesus calming the storm was one of awe for his divine presence. This is contrasted with Herod's fear of John the Baptist, because he knew him to be a 'righteous and holy man.' It differs from the fear of people experienced by the chief priests, the scribes, and the elders. This is the kind of fear familiar to most politicians, an experience which has nothing to do with the fear of the Lord, or 'a holy fear.' In Christian literature, the awe or the fear of the Lord; the *timor Domini*, is rated amongst the Spirit's gifts (see Lash 2008:185). On the contrary, the fear of Herod upon hearing that Jesus is born in Bethlehem, or upon hearing reports that John the Baptist was drawing huge crowd in his sermons leading to baptism of many by him, is motivated by his ambition to power. King Herod takes all this news as a threat to his power security. It is an imagined fear, not a real one. This type of fear is not holy and does little to help inner growth (see Crosby 2008:48).

Born to be a Sign of Contradiction

Jesus Christ the founder of Christianity lived in Palestine at the time of great injustice. The Jews both men and women, were bound by fear of the Roman Empire. The colonized Jews were so oppressed. Within Judaism itself the people were burdened by many laws which seemed difficult to bear. The existence of classes in society with the poor and slaves at the bottom, made those who had nothing in society to have no chance at all for a bright future. Jesus came in public to challenge the Empire and the hypocrisy of religious establishments. He began his ministry at the moment when John the Baptist who criticized King Herod openly is put into prison (see Mk 1:14). Jesus' radical way to bring truth forward in order to present God's will makes him a "sign of contradiction" and eventually his life security is taken away through crucifixion.

Just as when the prophecy of John the Baptist was silenced by imprisonment paving way to the rise of another critical voice, the history of Christianity is enriched by stories of persons who are "signs of contradiction." One who is a "sign of contradiction" to the world today is Pope Benedict XVI. In his book *Cardinal Ratzinger, the Vatican's Enforcer of the Faith*, John L. Allen Jr., expresses his admiration of the man about whom he writes, as one born to be a sign of contradiction. He describes Cardinal Joseph Ratzinger as a man of fidelity to what he thinks is true according to Church's teaching. The honesty of the man, who is now Pope, drives Allen to confirm to his readers that he cannot hesitate to choose Ratzinger as his personal confessor. An American scholar David F. Forte ascribed the same concept to Joseph Ratzinger when he writes, 'in an impious age, we need persons, including intellectuals, who are signs of contradiction. We need a Martin Niemöller, a Natan Shcharansky, a Joseph Ratzinger. As Simon predicted, Christ himself became the sign of contradiction to an impious age' (Forte 2007:41).

This is true in so far as Pope Benedict XVI is concerned. He has never hesitated to speak out when he thinks what is right and true. In 1996, he gave a book – length interview which was translated in English as Salt of the Earth. In it 'he expressed doubt as to whether Islam could be reconciled with Western–style democratic pluralism' (Allen, Jr 2009:119). Joseph Ratzinger also 'irked some Muslims by his opposition to Turkey's candidacy to join the European Union' (Allen, Jr 2009:119). Despite irking opinions such as pointed by Allen, the question about the security of the Cardinal never appears to be of much concern. It is coming today as the man holds the office as head of the universal Church and successor of Peter.

Perhaps the most awkward moment in the life of the then Cardinal Joseph Ratzinger was in the aftermath of the publication of the Declaration *Dominus Iesus* on 6th August 2000, the feast of the Transfiguration of the Lord. By this Declaration, the Congregation of the Doctrine of Faith of which Joseph Cardinal Ratzinger was its prefect, sought to defend what is absolutely central and primary in Christianity, that Christ himself, is the unique saviour of humankind. The release of this document created mixed feelings. The Declaration *Dominus Iesus* was severely criticized by some Catholic theologians engaged in ecumenical and interreligious dialogue. Some theologians were afraid that the document was a "public relations disaster" (*The Tablet*) for many feared the harm it would do to the vision of Vatican Council II, which in view of the decree *Nostrae aetate* has paved the way for the Church to engage in dialogue with the world. Thus some

Catholic theologians in Europe described *Dominus Iesus* in terms such as "offensive," "insensitive," "archaic and outdated" (Mannion 2007:83). In Germany, the document was often referred as "Dominus Joseph," to indicate that this document represented the mind of the cardinal and not of the Church (see Baum 2005:119).

In fact the outrage which came as a result of the publication of this document extended beyond the Roman Catholic Church. It made Protestants feel inferior compared to their Roman Catholic counterparts. Many felt that the document had suggested that their churches were purely sociological entities, not mediators of salvation. Ecumenically engaged personalities expressed shock at the language used in the document. The Reverend Ellen Wondra, an Anglican involved in the Catholic-Anglican dialogue, dismissed *Dominus Iesus* as "part of the era of mutual polemics among churches rather than an era of reconciliation and greater communion" A Lutheran ecumenist, Michael Root took a similar view, suggesting that the declaration put the Catholic Lutheran dialogue "back where we were thirty years ago." The General Secretary of the Lutheran World Federation, Dr. Ishmael Noko, spoke of his "dismay and disappointment" that the document ignored the labour of many years' positive dialogue between the Catholic and Lutheran churches, adding that it also overlooked the language used to describe Lutheran ecclesia communities in the 1999 Catholic-Lutheran "Joint Declaration on justification," which refers to them as "churches" (Mannion 2007:85). The heated reaction about the document *Dominus Iesus* saw the World Alliance of Reformed Churches threatening to withdraw from scheduled talks with the Catholic Church.

In interreligious dialogue, matters were not different. The Jewish community feared that through the publication of *Dominus Iesus,* the Roman Catholic Church was pushing them to the valley of darkness in Sheol! (see Baum 2005:119). Some Jewish groups wanted to cease all interfaith dialogue with the Catholic Church. Muslims voiced out their dissatisfaction and accused the Roman Catholic Church of "double standards" and logical inconsistencies in the document, which saw Islam as somehow defective, yet also a means to closer unity with God. The media was as usual, at the frontline onslaught. The *Los Angeles Times* for example, misrepresented the teaching of *Dominus Iesus* in a page-one headline, "Vatican Declares Catholicism Sole Path to Salvation," while another newspaper ran a cartoon of John Paul II, with arms raised, under the caption "We're Number One!" (Weigel 2010:249). Indeed many people thought that the Holy See was bypassing the spirit of Vatican II centred on communion and the idea of the people of God.

We have given informative evidence of the turmoil which occurred after the release of *Dominus Iesus* not to dismiss the relevance of this Instruction. The document is very relevant and in harmony with Roman Catholic tradition. It was approved by the late Pope John Paul II, who in person took efforts to clarify why the document was necessary in the aftermath of its criticism. *Dominus Iesus* was also recommended positively by some prominent cardinals and bishops. There were also a good number of theologians who gave credit to the document. The intention of producing the responses above is to help our readers understand the stormy situation which developed after the presentation of the curial document. The prefect of the Congregation of the Doctrine of the Faith then must have probably made a noted group of "enemies" who did not like his instructions. Despite the negative climate assassination of the cardinal was not in their minds, however.

Among the negative effects which came with the war against terrorism after the September 11, 2001 attacks was the idea that Islam was under attack by the West. The tactics advocated by militants were symptomatic of a greater difficulty with global security. There were some negative trends among radical Muslims to attack the Vatican and the Pope, considering the head of the Roman Catholic Church as sponsoring crusade campaigns against the spread of Islam. The Declaration on *Armed Struggle against Jews and Crusaders* which is signed by leaders of Al-Qaeda (the deceased Osama bin Laden and Ayman al – Zawahiri) and other militant organizations, pronounced that the use of armed forces is necessary. The Declaration makes it clear that to resort to armed force is the right and duty of all Muslims, wherever they are situated. It also affirms that such force may be directed at any and all targets, including those ordinarily considered "civilian" (see Kelsay 2010: 233). The threat posed by Islamic militants puts the lives of global leaders at risk. The situation is delicate particularly for leaders who are prophetic and vocal, those whom we consider to be a sign of contradiction to the world such as the Pope is.

The Papacy that began at the Time of Global Violence

The Pontificate of Benedict XVI began in May, 2005. Peter Seewald an informed journalist knew well what had taken place since Joseph Cardinal Ratzinger was installed on the Chair of Peter. The beginning of his office had been a difficult one. His papacy began at a fearful time in the Western world. The year before in 2004, there was a terrorist attack in Madrid and in the same year, another terrorist attack hit London at this point he had only been Pope for three months. To narrate a little bit the intensity of the violence, let us move on.

On March 11, 2004, four commuter trains were heading towards the Atocha Station in Madrid. The terrorists had hidden explosives inside the moving train. A total of thirteen improvised explosive devices had been carefully stocked on board the trains. The train attendants never noticed the danger; neither did the passengers. After a while, ten of them exploded, killing almost two hundred commuters. Police mounted an intensive investigation. Twenty-nine suspects were charged with conspiracy in the attacks. Most of those apprehended were originally from Maghreb country, notably Morocco, but have been naturalized in Spain (see Juergensmeyer 2008:174).

On November 2, of 2004, the 26-year-old Mohammed Bouyeri, belonging to the Muslim community in Amsterdam, attacked the Hollandaise film producer Theo Van Gogh as he was riding on his bicycle through the streets of Amsterdam. The filmmaker was shot several times with a pistol killing him instantly. After the assassination, Mohammed Bouyeri mutilated Van Gogh's body, leaving two messages on his body, explaining the motive for the murder. The aggressor took this drastic measure because the filmmaker had produced the film entitled *Submission* which presented Muslim men as oppressors of Muslim women. In addition, Mohammed Bouyeri committed the massacre to protest against the government for allowing the desecration of Islamic values in public. The assassin was found guilty and was sentenced to life imprisonment (see Juergensmeyer 2008:170).

The 2005 London terrorist attack came as if to remind the Pope, that he was beginning his ministry like Jesus did in a very fearful period. During morning rush hour on July 7th, four bombs which extremists had hidden in backpacks were ignited by suicide bombers. Three were detonated on underground subway trains within fifty seconds of each other, the fourth exploding a little time later causing widespread panic and commotion near Tavistock Square. The death toll of commuters was estimated to be over fifty (see Juergensmeyer 2008:174).

There was an outbreak of volcanic anger throughout the whole Muslim world. The catalyst was the publication of a series of cartoons in the Copenhagen newspaper *Jyllands-Posten* in September 2005. One of the cartoons portrayed the Prophet Mohammed wearing a turban in the shape of a bomb, the fuse lit and sputtering. Most of the men were shown with large noses, wearing beards and turbans. As newspapers circulated, the Muslim community became impatient. They protested angrily concerning the insults against their religion and their Islamic faith. Their rage amplified the global interest about the issue and the press coverage got a wide spread not only in the West but also in global South. The cartoons were reprinted in dozens of newspapers in fifty countries (see Juergensmeyer 2008:171).

The cartoon controversy entered Muslim dominated countries. It blasted into an outrage and called for retaliation. Amplifiers in mosques loudly send the message in public against the press and the Swedish cartoonist claiming for a *fatwa* against his head. According to many Muslims, this was a deliberate attempt to downgrade Prophet Mohammed and humiliate the Muslim population altogether. In February 2006, in the wake of the controversy, protests erupted in Pakistan, Indonesia, and Nigeria where about 200 people were killed. In Benghazi (Libya) extremists invaded the Franciscan monastery and killed six friars. A Turkish teenager killed a priest at the altar in the port city of Trabazon. Danish embassies were set on fire in Syria and Lebanon. Over 130 people were killed in the violence that took place in these countries. There was a widespread boycott of Danish goods in Muslim countries which reduced export to those countries by 15 percent, costing over 130 million euros in sales (see Juergensmeyer 2008:171).

In the following year 2006, British security officials succeeded to halt another plan to attack the country. The security personnel arrested a dozens Muslim extremists who had plotted to blow up British and American passenger planes. The planners had intended to use common electronic devices such as cell phones and iPods to detonate liquid explosives that would have brought down as many as ten planes (see Juergensmeyer 2008:175).

In the same year, the Pope's life was publicly threatened by Muslim extremists following a lecture he gave at Regensburg University in September 2006. Pope Benedict XVI produced a quotation from the Byzantine Emperor, Manuel II Paleogus. He said, "show me just what Mohamed brought that was new, and there you will find things only evil and inhuman, such as his command to spread by the sword the faith he preached." All major religions find that its radical movements share one thing: they dislike intellectuals and do not have patient to dialogue with them. The Pope made the quotation to an exclusive intellectual audience, but the emotion and uproar in the Muslim world failed to grasp what the Pope had been addressing and neither did they understand the context. The Muslim intellectuals however, did understand the Pope well, and took no offensive.

The situation remains delicate. Everywhere there is insecurity. The danger is not only from outside Christianity but also from within. Some Christian progressive Pentecostals tend to hate institutionalism of the Church. The Pope is considered a custodian of an institutional structure of the Body of Christ. Some people from sects even go further to look at the Pope as "an agent of Satan" who is to be attacked. 'The Pope had been thought of as "unseen, ghost-like enemy, lurking behind clouds of wicked incense in a satanic southern city called Rome' (Corren 2011:3).

The West is becoming increasingly secular. To be a Christian is considered by many as a private matter. The Church's influence in public seems to be diminishing. There is a new attitude among many people criticizing the Church's authority. Many Christians think that one can belong to Jesus without giving loyalty to an institutionalized church community! Moral and doctrinal statements of the Church are viewed negatively by some Catholic faithful. The hate towards the Church hierarchy and Roman authorities is one of the puzzling features of postmodernism. It is in the midst of such climate that concern about the security of the Pope should be raised.

The "YES" and "NO" of the Pope

Of all the responses the Pope has given to the questions levelled at him by Peter Seewald, two of the responses are the shortest. The first one makes an affirmation "Yes" to what the Pope is asked. The second one is negation, which states "No" to the question posed and is found in the second part. What one will find striking in studying the "Yes" and "No" of the Pope is that, he answers 20 times with the affirmation "Yes," but only once his response "Yes" stands alone without further clarification. On its part the answer "No" repeats 10 times, but only once does the answer "No" stand as it is without further elaboration. The Pope proves in giving affirmative "Yes" and "No" that his mind is clear and the position he takes in answering this questions is unequivocal.

Analysis of the "Yes" Reply

In the secular world the reply "Yes" has been popularized by President Barack Obama. In his 2008 election campaign the American president introduced as his motto "Yes, we Can" which immediately became a mantra among different movements to press for change.

We read the "Yes" answer in the book *Light of the World: the Pope, the Church, and Signs of the Times*, this time not by a politician, a rhetorical campaigner, but from a pastor, a man of moral and spiritual stand. The question that leads the Pope to give a straightforward answer "Yes" is the one concerning his interest in sports. As it is clear to everybody, sports have become a phenomenon in the contemporary world. Peter Seewald asks if the Pope thinks like Churchill: "No Sports?!" The response is simply "Yes." The Holy Father, however, does not clarify further. He makes his position.

This position of Pope Benedict XVI does not mean that he is absolutely against sports. If by his affirming "Yes" he meant that he is completely against sports, he could be contradicting himself. He could not have welcomed the Germany World Cup Organizing Committee which visited him at the Vatican to receive his pontifical blessing in October 2005, for example. The delegation was led by Franz Beckenbauer and Rudi Voller. It presented to the Pope the *Logo of the World Cup Finals* which took place in Germany in 2006. The negation against sports would be a frustration to many young priests and chaplains in secondary schools, who mobilize young people to take part in sports to build character and a sense of community. It could also sound as an embarrassment to the *Association of Catholic Priests Football Players*, who in 2009 presented Pope Benedict XVI with a jersey, courteously recognizing him as member of their team. The jersey carried his name *Benedetto*. Moreover, that could mark a departure from his predecessors, especially the Blessed John Paul II whose sportsmanship spirit earned him the title as "God's Athlete" and Pope Pius XII who is known as

"Friend of Sports." We can conclude from the above consideration that Pope Benedict XVI is not advocating a *spiritual fundamentalism*, a tendency to think that sports and recreation only distract from meditation and contemplation. For people with such mentality, doing sports is useless and a waste of time. From the answer "No" the Pope does not take side with the *sports mania* group either. The concept of *sports mania* applies to persons, who are totally absorbed with sports to the extent that they think always of sports, talk day and night about sports, and practice sports quite often. They have no spare time for worship services and spiritual meditation!

The challenge is always to try be balanced and avoid extremes. Unfortunately, many Christians view sports and games in a negative light. From Christian tradition, theology of Latin Fathers such as Tertullian, St. Jerome and St. Augustine has been cautious about sports as gateways to pleasure. The Manichean heresy of St. Augustine's time as it should be recalled condemned the body, believing it to be bad.

The first centuries of Christianity associated sports with evils hence games and sports were regarded as the work of Satan. This negative perception of sports was prompted above all by way in which the Roman and Greek Olympic ceremonies were officiated. These ceremonies and the feasts that manifested them were accompanied by the invocation of pagan gods. Victories were cheered by invocations to the deities. Those who emerged victors accomplished their victories by killing their victims. The cruel treatment of weak opponents in sports also facilitated its rejection in Christianity. In the year 393 AD emperor Theodosius, who was converted to Christianity, at the request of Bishop Ambrosius of Milan, published a decree to suspend all sporting activities in his empire (see Nyenyembe 2010:41). Hence, the Christian tradition has inherited a negative view about sports. Sports and recreation have been understood as channelling secularism and permissiveness.

We find even today some people within the Church, who are associating sports with mammon, and self pride. Taking part in sports is also thought by many to be a deterrent in study. Some Catholic bishops in Tanzania, for example, in the early 1990s instructed rectors of their seminaries to pull out from national secondary school sports competitions (*UMISETA*), fearing that taking part of seminarians in such competitions might conflict with their academic, religious and spiritual formation (see Nyenyembe 2010:15).

We can understand, then, that the Pope is not against sports as such. He is aware however, of the contemporary attitude that tends to elevate sports to the realm of religion with talented sportsmen being revered as idols. The Pope's absolute "Yes" in opposition to sports needs to be clarified. The Pope is not sports-phobic or fearful of sports but rather is against sports-theism, notably an attitude of revering sports as if they were a kind of spiritual medicine for contemporary human restlessness. In this sense sports may be used as diversion from life problems. The Pope refuses the false security that is evident in the mushrooming of fitness studios and gyms. Now let us move to his "No" reply

Testimony of Christian Courage

Asked if he is afraid of an assassination attempt, the Pope does not shoot back with questions like, "afraid of whom?" or "for what reason should they target me?" and queries of that nature. The "No" response of the Holy Father shows a clear position. It reflects a mature standing of a Christian believer in the face of threat. The Pope responds "No" as a Christian believer should. St. Paul admonishes us to be firm, so that when we say "Yes" it should be a bold affirmation. Equally when we answer "No" it should be a firm one (see 2 Cor 1:17-22). Every baptized Christian has received a Spirit, not of fear but of freedom. The Christian believer is warned in the Gospel, "Do not fear those who kill the body but cannot kill the soul (Mt 10:28, Lk 12:4). In reading Psalms, the Christian believer finds out that the Psalmist's life, too, had been threatened. But God's hand is powerful. The Psalmist prays, "Even though I walk through the valley of the shadow of death, I fear no evil, for you are with me. Your rod and your staff give me courage" (Ps. 23:4). We can be assured from these few lines above, that the Pope's "No" against any threat towards his life in defending the Christian truth is already linked with his baptismal mandate as a Christian believer. The premise here is that a human person should have no anxiety when it comes to defending the truth in matters of morals and faith. The "No" of the Holy Father shows he fears only the Lord.

The response "No" given by the Pope discloses his clear understanding of what it means to wear the shoes of the fisherman. Like St. Peter, all the apostles are called to follow the footsteps of the Lord. St. Paul puts it, "For I think that God has exhibited us apostles as last of all, as though sentenced to death, because we have become a spectacle to the world, to angels and to mortals" (1 Cor. 4:9). It is in the competence of the apostles to defend the truth and ensure that the will of God prevails over human ambitions. This is what Peter and John fulfil when the Scribes and the elders of the people ordered them not to preach about Jesus Christ, "But Peter and John answered them, 'whether it is right in God's sight to listen to you rather than to God, you must judge for we cannot keep from speaking about what we have seen and heard'" (Acts 4:19-20).

Pope Benedict's "No" to fear against assassination plot pertains to the nature of his office. There is in this "No" an ecclesial dimension. The Church has a prophetic mission, and as such She is not afraid of those who threaten her. 'Fearlessness and inner freedom are qualities we associate with prophets- those in every age who are bold enough to speak out when everyone else remains silent' (Nolan 2009:28). The Church does not originate from a human creativity but from God. It is destined to serve the will of Him not of evil powers. She is not to be deterred by human threats to her mission. In his book *Values of Time* he wrote while still a cardinal insisting on the disposition to be ready to die if it is about to fulfil the will of God:

> The faith of the New Testament acknowledges not the revolutionary but the martyr, who recognizes both the authority of the state and its limits. His resistance consists in doing everything that serves to promote law and ordered life in society, even when this

means obeying authorities who are indifferent or hostile to his faith; but he will not obey when he is commanded to do what is evil, to oppose the will of God. He is not the resistance of active force, but the resistance of one who is willing to suffer for the will of God (Ratzinger 2006:21).

Thus, finally one finds that the answer "No" has a catechetical function. The vocation of the Successor of Peter is to confirm his brothers and sisters in the faith (see Lk 22:32). At this time of history, not only is the security of the Pope, one of the major challenges to the Church, but also the religious freedom and security of many Christians is at stake. In places where Christians are a minority, in countries like Iraq and Pakistan they are persecuted. Christians are not free to practice their faith in public. Their very lives as believers, is threatened by death. To these Christians, one seeks to know what should be their attitude towards their persecutors. In fact while they should struggle for religious freedom, neither should they opt for violence nor fear assassination attempts orchestrated to threaten them. The answer of the Pope has a global dimension. The Christian faithful should be free from all the threats militating against them such as the right to practice one's faith. The right of Christians to witness what they believe has to go with the right of non-Christians to do the same.

There is a lack of courage among many Christians. 'So our society needs a strong dose of Christian courage, but the church does not always offer it' (Radcliffe 2005:71). Courage is a quality of the heart; it is a *fortitude mentis*, the capacity to see things as they are, to face the danger with a steadfast spirit, and to recognize human vulnerability. The answer "No" to fear for an assassination attempt is a brave response. Most Christians are afraid of things that are trivial and that are not a danger for the soul. Many people are haunted by fears that are unfounded (see Radcliffe 2005:73). In the face of insecurity today, Catholics need the virtue of courage. Fear in this case does not serve the pursuit of truth, but condemns us to servitude.

The "no" attitude to those who threaten to eliminate Christians based on what they uphold in matters of faith and morals may help to moderate the proper response of the Christian faithful. In face of life threat from those who target Christians the response may be either to flee away or to fight back. We learn from the Gospels that Jesus the non violent preacher proposes another way. Taking the path of violence by fighting back is not what he suggests either. Fleeing and leaving fellow Christians being butchered without a critical voice to defend them is not helpful. Jesus proposes to the Christian to turn the other cheek (see Mt. 5:43). 'To turn the other cheek is to prevent him from hitting you the same way again. It is not to run or to acquiesce, but rather to signal to the aggressor that you refuse to accept the set of assumptions that have made his aggression possible' (Barron 2011:50). It is a willingness to die for truth while remaining critical to the evil.

Such a willingness to risk death for the global service of humanity would certainly constitute a major inspiring challenge, no matter how talented the person...This new vocation of the global religious-based international servant of humanity could inspire a new generation of young people to live out their faith in situations that would be more, rather than less, demanding than that of facing the lions in the Roman Coliseum...For the Christian, then, the ultimate goal is not martyrdom but the love of Christ and of all other persons for whom Christ died (Hanson 2011:225).

To conclude this chapter we can say that human responsibility as the Pope portrays in the *Light of the World*, requires a life guided by conscience. One has not to move like wind simply following what the others are doing. Everyone who is guided by freedom and free will has to say "Yes" to something because she/he is convinced of its intrinsic value. Similarly one has to say "No" once he/she is clear of its intrinsic evil. The challenge today is to identify "false securities" which leads the Christians to go astray. This is necessary, because many people are afraid to take sides and to make their position because they fear for their lives. We can say that a lot of people today are at home with "face-book" yet are unaware of "faith-book."

2

In the shoes of the Fisherman

The title frequently used in the Roman Catholic Church in addressing the Pope is that of the "successor of Peter." This title designates the Bishop of Rome to the Petrine ministry. As "successor of Peter" the Pope walks in the shoes of the Galilean fisherman. While this understanding is widely accepted in Catholic tradition, what many Catholics seem not to be aware is that the title "successor of Peter" does not offer an assurance for security. The situation of insecurity is typical to anyone who claims to be Jesus' disciple (see Mk 9:34-36). St. Peter and St. Paul provide us with clear orientation for being Christ's followers without security such as the one which is offered by worldly powers.

Unfortunately, from the time of reformation the title "successor of Peter" has been used mainly in relation to the juridical and pastoral authority of the Pope as exercised in a perfect society, the Church. Popes have been studied much more as custodians of "heavy duty" keys and possessors of absolute and infallible words. The true humanity of a fallible leader has been eclipsed by an imagination of an unerring authority. In putting much emphasis on juridical power and authority of the Roman Pontiff, the truth about the insecurity of the Pope has not been out rightly brought forward.

The fact, however, is that the Petrine ministry is transferred to the current Pope from someone whose discipleship is a story of insecurity. One of the incidents which show this reality is at the time when Jesus hears that his friend Lazarus has fallen deeply sick. He tells his disciples that they should set out for Judea again. The apostles are not happy for they know that there is no security there at all. This is their reaction, "Rabbi, the Jews were just now trying to stone you, and are you going there again?" (Jn 11:7).

Let us closely look at Peter himself. He is just a human person, fallible and prone to commit errors. Verbally he is outspoken, open minded and, yet at times make wrong decisions. Psychologically, he is emotional by reacting to external threats with fear thus he could run away like many others. He faces the enemies of Jesus with aggression. Economically, he belongs to the lower class, the *anawim*; people without much who look at God, as refuge. We read in the Bible that while proposing that Jesus and the three disciples should remain at the place of Transfiguration his proposal is turned down. When walking on the water to follow Jesus; Peter stumbles and begins to drown. This is a person who rejects the idea of Jesus going to Jerusalem to suffer and die for others. In addition, St. Peter seeing the trouble which Jesus is about to face defends his master by striking the ear of the servant of the high priest, an act that meets strong reprimand from Jesus. Furthermore, we read that when he was recognized as one of Jesus' disciples, Peter categorically refuses any knowledge about the person. Interestingly, even as the head of the community of Christians in Rome, facing a difficult situation of persecutions he decides to run away in order to find a safer place somewhere else.

Guided by what the Holy Scripture informs us about him and responding to the context of violence and rebellion we face today, the title "successor of Peter" needs to be approached in view of security and peace. In a situation of insecurity for Christians the world over, the temptation is to take the sword and defend ourselves just as Peter did. We have to study what is the position of Jesus in face of violence that threatens his disciples. Moreover, it is helpful to look at a series of imprisonment which Peter endured, and his final attempts to run away from persecutions. This will help us as support at the time of difficulties to stick to unwavering perseverance amidst all insecurities.

Galilean Man designated as Rock

The Church which Jesus had founded was entrusted to the Galilean fisherman. The ordinary man from the Sea of Galilee is the brother of Andrew, also a fisherman. He was among the first to be called by Christ as they were fishing along the sea shore (see Mt 4:18-22; Mk 1:16-20; Lk 5:1-11). After the calling, Peter left his nets and followed Jesus. Though he was originally named Simon, it seems that Jesus gave him an Aramaic name, Cephas, which meant "Rock." "And Jesus answered him, 'Blessed are you, Simon son of Jonah! For flesh and blood has not revealed this to you, but my Father in heaven.' And I tell you, you are Peter, and on this rock I will build my church" (Mt 16:17-18). The choice of this name is significant for the role which St. Peter is called to play in the Church.

In Palestine during the time of Jesus, rocks were used for a variety of purposes. In times of danger and in war soldiers covered themselves with rocks. These helped them to dodge the enemy soldiers. Some rocks were shaped like caves which made hiding from the enemy useful. When King Saul, out of jealousy, had sought to murder David, the young man run away and took refuge in caves (see 1 Sam 23:28; 24:1-7). We see that the name "rock" given to Simon Peter gives him with a mandate to protect and confirm members of the Church. Later Jesus will tell Peter, "but I have prayed for you that your own faith may not fail; and you strengthen your brothers" (Lk 22:32).

Rocks are used as construction materials. The rock foundations of buildings and houses resisted natural disasters. These foundations were made up of pieces of stones broken from the rocks. Luke narrates about the believer who laid a strong foundation on which his faith is deeply founded. "That one is like a man building a house, who dug deeply and laid the foundation on rock; when a flood arouse, the river burst against that house but could not shake it, because it had been well built" (Lk 6:48). From this understanding St. Peter is the person who acts as stone foundation for the Church. The

Petrine ministry rallies the faithful always to refer to the rock foundation, that is, the essentials of the Catholic faith.

Finally, rocks served as a source of water. When the Israelites were in the wilderness and complained about the shortage of water, God told Moses, "I will be standing there in front of you on the rock at Horeb. Strike the rock, and water will come out of it, so that the people may drink" (Ex. 17:6-7). In the Book of Exodus there are two great events where water is the main feature. The first is the passage through the Red Sea and the second is the water that came out of the rock. On all these occasions water plays quite different roles as well. In the first case, man entered the water; in the second, water entered man. The water of the Red Sea saved some and caused others to perish. It was the instrument of God's punishment (Cantalamessa 2003: 148). The water of the rock performed a different function: it quenched the people's thirst, restored their strength and enabled them to move ahead with their journey. In fact, according to rabbinic tradition, repeated by Saint Paul, the rock from which the water gushed "followed" or "accompanied" the people on their journey through the desert from that day onward (see 1 Cor 10:4). The two waters were interpreted, more precisely, in connection with the action of the Holy Spirit in baptism and in the Eucharist: "For in the one Spirit we were baptized and in the Eucharist: 'For in the one Spirit we were all baptized into one body,...and we were all made to drink of one Spirit" (1 cor 12:13).

Water is a crucial element in the sacramental life of the Christian faithful. On the cross Jesus shed blood and water as our source of life. Tertullian says; "never is Christ without water." The Petrine ministry has to make sure that the waters keep gushing from the rock. It is to ensure that the Church does not die of thirst. Catholics are familiar with the famous Easter period song; the *vidi aquae*, "I have seen the water at the right side of the Temple," taken from the vision of Ezekiel in the temple (see Ez. 47:1). This alludes to the foundation of the Church which is to become a gathering in the Spirit by the water of baptism. It is through the water new members are to be born in the Spirit. Moreover, through the blessing with the water the people of God are graced with life to the full (see Jn 10:10). Those newly born in the water through the Spirit are indeed temple of the Holy Spirit. The reader is invited here to recall the promise of Jacob following the dream, "...and this stone, which I have set up for a pillar, shall be God's house" (Gen. 28:22). It is endowed upon the Petrine ministry and all the ordained ministers to baptize and therefore, to welcome new members into the Church.

St. Peter's call to be a shepherd comes after the account of a miraculous catch of fish. After a night in which the disciples had let down their net without success; they see the Risen Lord on the shore. He tells them to let down their nets once more, and the net became so full that they could hardly pull it in. "And although there were so many, the net was not torn" (Jn 21:11). The story of Peter's calling to shepherd the flock by the Lord at the Sea of Tiberias, coming at the end of Jesus' earthly ministry corresponds very well with the account of Simon Peter's calling together with his brother Andrew at the Sea of Galilee. There too, the disciples had caught nothing the entire night. There too, Jesus had invited Simon once more to put out into the deep waters. And, Simon who was not yet called Peter gave his firm concession, "master, at your word I will let down the nets." And, then, following the conferral of his mission: "Do not be afraid. Henceforth you will be catching men" (Lk 5:1-11).

In his calling to become a disciple and to shepherd the sheep in the vineyard of the Lord, Peter is connected with water and the sea; and the activity of fishing. The fishing activity provides enough resources to discover the temperament of Simon Peter. Fishing is an activity which is tedious and risky. Oceans, seas and lakes are known for turbulent waves accompanied by strong winds. The biblical Sea of Galilee and its immediate basin are entirely contained in the deep and very narrow tectonic trough of the Jordan Valley, itself an element of the Great Rift Valley going down all the way to East Africa. All the lakes formed along this valley are reputed to have occasional stormy waters. The sporadic and chaotic stormy winds endanger the security of fishermen. At one moment Jesus was travelling with his disciples in the boat and he was sleeping. At once a "great windstorm arose and the waves beat into the boat, so that the boat was already being swamped. But he was in the stern, asleep on the cushion; and they woke him up and said to him, 'Teacher, do you not care that we are perishing?" (Mt 8:23-27, Mk 4:35-41, Lk 8:22-25). In fact the scene of calming the storm provides an opportunity for the disciples to trust the Master. He rebuked them in turn: "Why are you afraid? Have you no faith?" (v.40). 'The term *deiloi*, meaning afraid, is very strong, expressing total disarray. During the storm the disciples had failed to trust God (v. 38). Jesus' tranquil sleep should have been a sign for them. He accused them of having no trust in him' (Harrington 2010:85).

Fishermen live in insecurity. They are surrounded by stories of evil forces moving along the waters especially during the night. These bizarre creatures popularly known in Kiswahili as *majini* (creatures of waters), which are ghosts plying the waters are said to hate human beings and always intend to do them harm. Fishing in the night remembering such stories adds to their anxiety. When the disciples were fishing and suddenly saw Jesus walking on the water they became afraid, for they thought he was a kind of *mzimu* or *jini*, a ghost, "But when they saw him walking on the sea, they thought it was a ghost and were terrified" (Mk 6:49). From his calling as a fisherman, Peter is overcome with fear. But his background encourages him to put his trust in Jesus.

It is this trust and open mindedness which is characteristic of many people who are born along the waters, possibly related to the nature of fishing (one has to go fishing in some cases almost naked). For that, Peter is outspoken and open and could confess that "Jesus is Christ, Son of the Living God." And when Jesus began to teach his disciples that he would suffer and die in Jerusalem and rise again on the third day, it is Peter the fisherman, who took him aside and rebuked him (see Mt 16:22; Mk 8:32). When Jesus said that Peter could not follow him now but would do so later, Peter asked: "Lord, why can't I follow you now? He was so eager to follow his master that he affirmed that he was willing to lay down his life for him (see Jn 13:36-37). Simon Peter trusted in the master so strongly that he did not accept that he could suffer. As a fisherman and later as a member of the body of disciples, Peter rejects the misery of insecurity. Life without security is a nightmare. He decides to differ with what Jesus proposes. Peter is not ready to be humiliated. This kind of wretchedness he lived as a fisherman already. Most people who depend on fishing experience economic difficulties. Thus, honesty compels him to reject Jesus' proposal. Peter, in both his profession as fisherman, and afterward as a disciple and leader of the community, is insecure. 'Until Peter followed Jesus to Jerusalem, witnessed from afar his condemnation and his crucifixion, and saw in person the resurrected Christ - only then could he begin to understand the call "follow me." It was a call that led him not to the majestic throne room of the Empire, but to the way of suffering servanthood, and only by that route to the life offered in the kingdom of God' (Camp 2008:58).

Peter's Sword and the Mind of Jesus

Just as Peter felt insecure in the past so are Christians today. In addressing injustice and violence in the world some Christians side with those who seek their rights by the use of violence, selecting some biblical passages like Matthew 10:34-35 "Do not think that I have come to bring peace to the earth; I have not come to bring peace, but a sword." There are still some Christian faithful including Catholics who support violence with the opinion that at the last supper Jesus told the twelve, "And the one who has no sword must sell his cloak and by one" (Lk 22:36). Some have recourse to the book of Revelation, where we read about the sword that gets out from the mouth of the Lord (see Rev. 19:15). Taking these passages literally may mislead, Christians have to grasp its spirit and the central message of it. Scripture scholars understand these statements differently. The first one in Mt. 10:34-35 "Do not think that I have come to bring peace on the earth; I have not come to bring peace, but a sword," the idea "sword" is a metaphor for how the truth of Jesus divides and polarizes people. It is used in a metaphorical manner 'for how the truth of Jesus divides and polarizes people. The metaphorical sword, in this case, is held by our enemies, often family members, but not by the disciples, who are hated because of His name (see Lk 21:7), and "marked out as undesirable"' (Garrity Ranaghan 2011:20). In the second statement spoken during the last supper, we can deduce that by stating that in their limited capacity they have two swords, the disciples seem to have completely misunderstood Jesus. They revealed in this case their hidden false image of a warrior messiah. The re-known biblical scholar Raymond Brown conceives that, 'the passage does not demonstrate that everyone should have a sword, but that everyone should be prepared...purse, bag, and sword are quasi symbolic ways of concretizing necessary readiness' (Brown 1994:689). We shall come to the third statement from the book of Revelation in following chapters.

The position of Jesus to non-violence is not ambiguous it is clear. Logically Jesus would not direct his disciples to prepare their sword ready, and then reprimand Peter not to use the sword against his enemies. The soldiers who were sent to arrest Jesus at Gethsemane met with a resistance. Peter tried to defend his master by drawing a sword and cutting off the ear of a servant of the high priest (see Jn 18:10). Jesus reprimanded Peter and through him all his disciples, "put your sword back into its place; for all who take the sword will perish by the sword" (Mt 26:52, Jn 18:10-11). The position of Jesus not to use violence matches with what is narrated in Matthew 5:39 where Jesus forbids his followers to answer violent action by violent action, and with Matthew 10:39 which encourages them to be willing to lose their lives for his sake (see Garrity Ranaghan 2011:20).

According to the Sermon on the Mount Jesus proposes to his disciples to turn the other cheek to the aggressor (see Mt 5:39), not intending his disciples to be submissive to violence. For some Christians the suggestion to turn the other cheek is one of the most provocative Bible verses. It is not to be forgotten that Jesus stands for peace not for violence. The peace which Jesus preaches is aimed at the restoration of order. The violence on the contrary, is an expression of the devil at work in the world. One of the biblical names for the devil is *ho diabolos*, which is derived from the concept *diabalein* (to bring disorder, to throw apart). The proposal that Jesus' disciples should turn the other cheek is very ideal for world peace. It 'is to prevent (the person) from hitting you the same way again. It is not to run or to acquiesce, but rather to signal to the aggressor that you refuse to accept the set of assumptions that have made his aggression possible. It is to show that you are occupying a different moral space' (Barron 2011:50). The Christian faithful knows that his/her dignity as God's child is not based on hitting back in kind to those who strike us but rather in following the mind of Christ. Catholics indeed all Christians should respond to violence in the same way as Jesus could do. At the cross while completely beaten and exhausted with no chance to come back to life, Jesus utters mercy, "Father forgive them; for they know not what they do" (Lk 23:34).

Jesus wanted to build a community which opts for peaceful dealing in face of hostile forces. It has to be understood that at the time of Jesus, the sword was a symbol of military strength. It guaranteed a security to the one who carried it, and expressed the power of the person who possessed it. Therefore the military generals and ruling class members carried the sword with them. When Jesus told his disciples not to use the sword even in the context of an aggressive attack by an enemy, it was a complete new idea. Jesus sought to establish a community that was vulnerable, that lived not on retaliation and a show of power but on serving the cause of peace. The Latin Fathers like Origen and Tertullian fully opposed Christians to take part in military operations insisting strongly that Jesus did not allow Peter to use the sword (see Perabo 2010:253)

To completely have no recourse to the use of the sword, sought to invite the new community to a way of becoming an offer. A new community founded by Jesus should not rely on a sword, and shun violence. Let us draw some insights from the encounter between David and Goliath in the Old Testament. During the fight between the two men, Goliath advances to encounter David arrogantly because he had a sword and a spear. But as he did so, David told him, "You come to me with sword and spear and Javelin; but I come to you in the name of the LORD of hosts, the God of the armies of Israel whom you have defied" (1 Sam 17:45). The lesson that comes to us in this episode is that even if David had no sword like Goliath, to the end Goliath the giant perishes with the same sword he used to humiliate the weak. "Then David ran and stood over the Philistine: he grasped his sword, drew it out of its sheath, and killed him; then cut off his head with it (1 Sam 17:51).

There is a spiritual lesson here. We should not think that David who represents a messianic figure was a bloodshed man. The death of Goliath on David's hands was permitted by the God of Israel, to show that he is a more powerful God than the gods of the Philistines. 'The duel between Goliath and David had multidimensional implications. It was both secular and religious…Religious in the sense that it involved the confrontation between the Israelite's strong monotheistic belief, and the pagan polytheism of the Philistines. Unlike other battles it was religious because the contenders invoked the gods. David made his recourse to the God of Israel. He made a public confession of his strong monotheistic belief' (Nyenyembe 2010:37). The killing of Goliath henceforth signified the triumph of monotheism. David himself is represented in others verses of the first book of Samuel to refuse to spill the blood of his enemy king Saul. Despite several attempts of the king to kill him, David, on the contrary, totally rejects the idea of killing Saul (see 1 Sam 24:1-25; 26:1-25).

To this development we do not intend to judge as irrational the Christians who advocate the use of violence. What we seek to underscore is the fact that the Christian faithful must understand the mind of the founder of Christianity well. In fact most of them have relevant reason when they want some justice be done which may imply the shedding of blood, for they may be tempted to think that prohibiting killing altogether is likely to allow the perpetuation of evils.

Prisoner in Maximum Security Jail

The community which Jesus visits at the Easter evening is shackled with fear. 'When it was evening on that day, the first day of the week, and the doors of the house, where the disciples had met, were locked for fear of the Jews, Jesus came and stood among them and said, "Peace be with you"' (Jn 20:19). The group of the disciples seem psychologically crippled. They are gathered in Jerusalem together with Peter and Mary, the mother of God, like a "little flock without security." It is a small congregation of "fearful remnants" who previously have deserted their master during his capture at Gethsemane. One of them, the leader, has denied the master three times and never appears at Calvary scene. Another disciple is reported rather than allowing himself to be captured when he was arrested, he manoeuvred them, and slipped from their hand without clothes (see Mk 14:52). Most of the disciple have run away afraid of being included in the persecution list before Pilate and the Sanhedrin. After a while as all of them recollect in the upper room, they are overrun by a "guilty conscience" with the exception of Mary and John the beloved disciple. No one else had courage to point a finger at the other one. Every one of them had fear; everyone had stories of feeling of brokenness during escape.

At Easter evening this community receives the peace of the Risen Lord, the healing within to restore the brokenness brought by fear. The Easter peace comes at full swing at the day of Pentecost. From this event the community is energized with divine power. What we find from the time of Pentecost onwards, is that the disciples start to pronounce with courage the great deeds the Lord has done to them. They witness to the Risen Lord, and assume with courage their mission to form the nations into discipleship.

The secular powers and some religious establishments in Jerusalem are worried about the new movement. The Easter community wins the hearts of many people as apostles are performing miracles, and converting thousands of them. This situation is judged as unacceptable by the high priests and the

Sanhedrin. Immediately, the community of disciples feels insecure. Peter and his community of believers recognize that their way of life is without security immediately after Pentecost.

The high priests and the Sanhedrin targets leaders of the movement to silence them. They are not permitted to preach the name of Jesus Christ, and are to refrain from doing wonders. That Peter is leader of the group and exhibits extraordinary courage to speak out and witnesses to the Resurrection of the Lord, arouses to anger the authorities in Jerusalem. They were astonished beyond measure that Peter and John who were uneducated and ordinary men, could excel in their testimonies of faith. So the Jewish tribunal in Jerusalem vied to decapitate the head of the movement. Peter and John were declared "prisoners," without being incarcerated (see Acts 4:1ff). The Jewish tribunal began harassing the community's leadership. This is how the military strategist has worked throughout world history. To halt the spread of movements which seem not to work in favour of the ruling class, the group leaders are usually targeted. In strikes, protests and demonstrations against states, institutions and schools, group leaders are always the focus, and end up falling victim to the cause. So Peter as leader of the primitive Church is deprived the status of "good citizen." He is considered a "prisoner" in other words a man deprived of security.

Since Peter and John are not incarcerated and put in prison this time, they continue to preach and do the work of the Lord. The Christians gather in communities to listen to the word from the apostles and share bread from their hands. The Christian faithful multiplied. The success of the apostles sounds the tone of alarm to establishments in Jerusalem.

The community of believers find themselves at a new development of the level of insecurity. Now the persecution of the Christians begins. Some of them are forced out of Jerusalem to Diaspora to save their lives. Others are put into prison. At this level, Peter is put but in a minimum security prison, in public prison (see Acts 5:1ff). The intention here is to ensure that the Christian believers feel that they are not secure now that their leaders are locked behind bars. Usually, the public prisons contain more inmates than maximum security jails. By putting Peter in public prison, probably the Sanhedrin wished to diffuse the news about Peter's imprisonment to a wider audience. The placing of Peter behind bars is designed to try to prevent those who follow him as their leader and indeed all the Christians not to preach in the name Jesus Christ. While in prison however, we are told that a miracle happens, the angel of the Lord opened the prison doors and let the prisoner free (see Act 5:19-20).

Coming to a more sophisticated development of insecurity at this stage persecutions are intensified. The primitive Christians are subjected to persecutions which left them insecure. Peter is practically "a wanted person." The authorities are determined to eliminate him. This is clear by the shrewd measures which Herod takes at this stage. First to warn all the believers he killed John (see Acts 12:1ff). The reader should notice that, it is at this stage that important personalities like Stephen are killed by stoning (see Acts 7:54-60). After the killing of John, Herod continued to humiliate Peter. He arrested him and this time did not place him in a public prison, but in a maximum security prison.

Normally, prisons are classified and arranged according to the provision of security level. "Maximum security is the most restrictive level of confinement and minimum security is the least restrictive' (North Carolina 2011). The prisoners confined at maximum security prisons are, 'the most dangerous inmates who are a severe threat to public safety, correctional staff, and other inmates' (North Carolina 2011). Imprisoned in the maximum prison denied Peter total freedom. He was watched over by four squads of soldiers. The reader should notice that it was not prison warders but soldiers. Now, this is like war against Christianity. The treatment Peter received was like that of a highly feared criminal. He was bound with two chains. Such strict incarceration diminished chances of his escape. The Christian believers completely lost hope of seeing Peter again.

The Book of Acts of the Apostles informs us of what came out at this stage. The community of believers prayed hard for him. The power of prayer and faith of the primitive Church worked. There were two unexpected events which took place on account of this. The angel of the Lord delivered Peter and set him free to the surprise of all the disciples. "When (Peter) knocked at the outer gate, a maid named Rhoda came to answer. On recognizing Peter's voice, she was so overjoyed that instead of opening the gate, she ran in and announced that Peter was standing at the gate. They said to her, 'You are out of your mind'" (Acts 12:12-17). Second, related to this event is the abrupt and dishonoured death of Herod, whose addiction to power led his followers to flatter him as a god, while he himself entertained the honours which God only deserves (see Acts 12:20-23). The miraculous release of Peter from the maximum prison, and the death of Herod offer a spiritual insight for us. God does not abandon those who revere Him and proclaim His Name. Finally it is God who offers true security. Peter as a freed man says; "Now I am sure that the Lord has sent his angel and rescued me from the hands of Herod and from all that the Jewish people were expecting" (Act 12:11). Those who think to provide security on their own, end up badly. The lesson from the downfall of Herod is inspirational. "On an appointed day Herod put on his royal robes, took his seat on the platform, and delivered a public address to them. The people kept shouting, 'The voice of a god, and not of a mortal!' And immediately, because he had not given the glory to God, an angel of the Lord struck him down, and he was eaten by worms and died" (Acts 12:21-23).

Flight from Persecutions: But *Quo Vadis?*

The persecutions of Christians did not end even with the death of Herod. As Christianity spread within the Roman Empire, Christians were considered to be enemies of the Empire. They were mistreated and persecuted. During the reign of Emperor Nero around the year 70 AD, the city of Rome was set on fire and to avoid his personal responsibility, he accused the Christians for the burning. In doing so he began severely persecuting those who claimed themselves to be Christians. The first martyrs of Rome, whom the Church honours on 30th June of every year, were massacred at this time.

The community of believers endured the harsh persecution with serenity and with prayer. They neither retaliated nor complained. In the face of severe humiliation the Christian faithful endured the sufferings inflicted to them with an amazing docility. The disciples were set apart as people of charity, forgiveness and peace. The *Letter to Diognetus* makes an assessment of the early Christians as people who "love all men, and by all men are persecuted. They are unknown, and still they are condemned; they are put to death, and yet are brought to life. They are poor, and yet they make many rich; they are completely destitute, and yet they enjoy complete abundance. They are dishonoured, and in their very dishonour are glorified…they are reviled, and yet they bless; when they are affronted, they still pay due respect. When they do good they are punished as evildoers; undergoing punishment, they rejoice because they are brought to life' (*Letter to Diognetus*, 5.10).

The persecution of the Christians continued to be magnified at an alarming proportion by Emperors Nero (54-68 AD) and Diocletian (250-268). The strategy of Nero was to completely wipe out Christianity from history. 'From the time of Nero it was the mere *nomen* of being a Christian that seems to have been sufficient reason to bring down the iron arm of Roman justice' (Cunningham 2011:10). In a film that shows the persecutions of the early Christians, the chief of protocol before the imperial palace whose name is Pedron discusses with Nero about the fate of the Christians. Nero is depicted as swearing that "I will deal with the Christians in a most brutal way to such an extent that history will not be able to prove that they ever existed." He is very serious with the statement, as the film moves on to present the intensified operation of persecution against the Christians.

At this difficult time Christians were cornered everywhere. The legend has it that Peter made a decision to run away from Rome to save his life. As he took flight, Peter meets Jesus on the Appian Way disguised as an old man: "And when he saw him, he said, 'Lord, where are you going?' And the Lord said to him, 'I go to Rome to be crucified.' And Peter said to him, 'Lord, are you being crucified again?' He said to him, 'Yes, Peter, I am being crucified again! Peter came to his senses, and having beheld the Lord ascending into Heaven, he returned back to Rome, rejoicing and glorifying the Lord, because he said, 'I am being crucified,' which was about to happen to Peter.

Christian tradition holds that Peter was arrested again, and after enduring persecution he was crucified. He rejected however, being crucified like Jesus Christ, and eventually was crucified upside down. This is how he was finally killed. As head of the college of apostles, he is depicted as a man without security. In his series of imprisonments, however, we see God's intervention to rescue him. We can be assured by such narratives that the angels of the Lord do not sleep. The guardian angels are ever awake and that is why we persevere amidst many dangers on the course of our lives.

Model of a Genuine Disciple

Perhaps one question which readers of this book may still have to ask after reading all the reflections concerning the insecurity of Peter is "How can a human person like Peter whose life is marked by insecurity be a source of security for the Church?" Does he really deserve to be seen as a "rock?" We do not hesitate to say that Peter deserves the title and the position. This is a man who exercises a deepened relationship with Jesus Christ.

A Sinner Who Admits Sins and Repents

Today than ever before we miss the word "sin" in public conversations. Concepts such as "sin," "hell" and "conscience" are not employed frequently. Hardly do we hear someone who wrongs another pleading for mercy with statements like "I have sinned please forgive me." Listen to BBC programmes like the "Hard Talk," for example, follow any programme in secular television channels and radios, you will rarely hear someone employing the word "sin." In the era which extols personal freedom, self autonomy, and self determination the word "sin" is completely dismissed. This has reduced interest to go to the sacrament of confession. The more people keep away from reconciling with God, the more they feel insecure. Modern secularism propels an ambiguous culture where people want to keep away from God. In trying to hide away from God they retreat into privacy and live inside compounds with steel consolidated gates to procure a self-made security. What these people neglect is the fact that God is omniscience for he knows better where we are and the profile record of our souls. And it is no wonder that, there are increasingly today a number of psychiatric cases, including depression. All over the world, but particularly in the developed West, many families are in difficult situation. Husbands, wives and children need concerted care from Church ministers for the turbulent climate within marriages. Violence, abuses and aggression at homes are hardly responded with the mind of Jesus. Generally speaking, in solving differences between married couples one finds lack of a spiritual will to forgive. Partners put trust to material security: such as house, work and salary, and legal support forgetting the spiritual course to follow a "downward movement" of humility. The logics of self righteousness and revenge do not extend to marriage commitments a chance. It facilitates marriage breakdown. Divorce and separation disrupt the harmony of families. What comes as a result is frustration. Frustrated persons may resort to excessive alcohol, too much smoking, and drug addiction and when all these do not work some of them attempts suicide. The fact that we tend to deny the true human nature of sin, and our calling to reconcile with God, fellow human beings and the whole creation, we risk more disappointments. The denial of truth about our being sinners does neither reward us with security nor help us to be sincere to our discipleship.

The fisherman of Galilee St. Peter the "rock" may offer a lesson here. At the occasion of the miraculous catch of fish, he just knelt down and confessed his imperfection. He and his fellow fishermen have become desperate and without energy left. They have spent the whole night without a catch. One can assume that the fishermen were tired and exhausted. They had given up a hope for the day. At the dawn of the day with sunshine penetrating the waters, an experienced fisherman like Peter knew that it was wastage of time to go fishing again. At this moment Jesus appears to them and commands them to try to lower the nets again. Listening and obeying are qualities which Peter portrays even at this difficult moment, "but at your command I will lower the nets" (Lk 5:5). Upon seeing Jesus his master, Peter overcomes an egoistic, relativistic attitude. He listens and obeys the Lord. He does not rely on his human experience alone. He trusts the words of Jesus. It pays off. The miraculous catch of fish humbles the man of Galilee. He feels unworthy and reacts "Depart from me, Lord, for I am a sinful man!" (Lk 5:8). This is a reaction of someone with strong faith, yet who is not proud but humble from within.

Another thrilling moment is after the capture of Jesus at Gethsemane. The soldiers brought Jesus in the courtyard of the high priest's house. Peter took courage to follow the soldiers while other disciples have run away. He joined the company of soldiers and workers inside. Three times he was spotted and told that he was one of those who belonged to the list of disciples. Peter denied all these times. The denials were punctuated by cock crows. Peter was brought to his senses and remembered what Jesus told him earlier on "Before the cock crows twice you will deny me three times." The reaction of Peter is very revelatory, we are told that "he went out and wept bitterly" (Mt 26:75). This is an allusion to the pains and tears which flow from Joseph eyes as he wept bitterly during the encounter with his brothers in Egypt (see Gen 45:2-3). He was deeply reminded of the sins his brother had committed earlier, intending to kill him, then selling him away, and finally cheating their father about his whereabouts.

Peter as someone confessing his sins and weeping for what he has done is a guide for all of us mortals. We are all sinners. Our daily experiences reveal the fact that we fall short of integrity in many things. To accept the state of our being sinners is not weakness; it is on the contrary a way to holiness. Acknowledging one's state of sin humbles and challenges the person to conversion. St. Ignatius of Loyola said that one of the greatest graces he had ever received was the charisma of the tax collector - the discovery that he was a sinner just like everyone else. During the middle Ages the time which St. Ignatius of Loyola lived, the Church emphasized much about the reality of human beings as sinners. At this time, a popular Christian spirituality began to underline strongly the importance of Jesus' sufferings, and putting stress on the practices of penitence, fasting and abstinence. This kind of spirituality was strongly lived among monks and nuns in monasteries. At the Cistercian monastery in Aldersbach near Regensburg (Bavaria region in Germany), there is a beautiful church building with definitive appearance in Baroque style. At the entrance door of the church is placed the statue of St. Peter and near this statue is a portrait of a cock. Underneath the statue is placed a penitential box image. At the opposite side parallel to where the image of St. Peter is, one can see the portrait of St. Mary Magdalena. Accordingly, these two figures have something in common to share with us. They are repentant sinners. The penitential box which is placed near Peter's image informs us of the fact that the admission of our sins, and ultimately reconciliation with God and those we have wronged is life towards perfection. Maria Magdalena and Peter are pardoned sinners who eventually are entrusted with the Easter kerygma. In the evening at Easter Sunday the risen Jesus commissions the apostles to forgive sins. Alas, we live at the time of history where the forgiving love of God is hardly appreciated anymore; we prefer to retaliate in kind while executing justice through violence.

A Disciple whose Life is built around Christ

The image of St. Peter as "rock" of the Church is cemented by the way his relationship with Jesus Christ is presented in the New

Testament. From his calling he is portrayed as someone who follows Christ closely. His relationship with the teacher is one of love, emotions and sometimes of tension. He is a disciple who likes to talk with the Lord and ask him question. His manner of discipleship is not that of a blind follower. The fisherman of Galilee navigates a radical way of discipleship. He is committed in his companionship with the Lord. He takes part in almost all important functions of Jesus earthly ministry. He poses questions and dialogues with the Lord to understand things better. St. Peter never takes things for granted. Perhaps it is because of his persistent curiosity he was able to identify Jesus. When Jesus wanted to know how people described him he called his disciples and asked them at Caesarea-Philippi, "Who do people say that I am?" The disciples gave a list of identities, like some say "John the Baptist, others Elijah, still others one of the prophets." Now Jesus wanted to know specifically from the inner cycle, the twelve, how they describe him. Peter responded on behalf of others, "You are the Messiah, the Son of the Living God" (Mt 16:16). Jesus was very much impressed with the confession of Peter. He proclaimed, "Blessed are you, Simon son of Jonah. For flesh and blood has not revealed this to you, but my heavenly Father" (Mt 16:17-18).

At the Sea of Tiberias after his resurrection Jesus converses with Peter. Three times Peter is asked repeatedly the same question, "do you love me?" It may be boring for someone who knows you already and for a long time, asking you the same question. The fisherman from Galilee never gets tired and assures Jesus Christ, "Lord, you know that I love you" (Jn 21:15, 16, 17). St. Augustine was the first to comment that the threefold statement of love was meant to counteract the threefold denial. 'Perhaps most tellingly here, Peter emerges as the archetype of the forgiven and commissioned church, for after each of his affirmations, Peter hears the command to "tend my sheep"' (Barron 2011:12).

St. Peter teaches us to value the conversion destined to renew one's life. It is a kind of life shaped by the power of the risen Lord. For that the Christian assumes the strength to witness the truth in the face of lies. We see Peter courageously telling the authorities in Jerusalem; "You, with the help of the wicked men, put him to death by nailing him to the cross" (Act 2:23). With prophetic honesty of a committed disciple he contrasts the actions of sinful persons with that of God. In view of his prophetic mission St. Peter draws a clear and sharp contrast between what the Jewish authorities have done and what God has done. "You killed him-but God raised him from the dead, freeing him from the agony of death, because it was impossible for death to keep its bold on him" (Acts 2:24). So, in contrast with the time before Jesus' passion and death, when he was against Jesus' proposal to endure sufferings and face death; after resurrection of the Lord, he is ready to die for the Lord. The act of going back to Rome and face difficulties is worthy emulating. His death as a martyr is what crowns him finally as a veritable rock of the Church. When St. Ignatius of Antioch was taken to Rome to be martyred in AD 107, he begged the Roman Christians not to try to save him, so that by dying he could become 'an intelligible utterance of God' (Raddcliffe 2005:70). Pope Benedict underscores an important point: 'it is not power, but love that redeems us! God, who became a lamb, tells us that the world is saved by the Crucified One, not by those who crucified him' (Benedict XVI 2005:193).

3

Targeting Popes

The chapter we have just finished reveals the insecurity that the apostles faced. Like Peter, his successors have experienced the same fate. Some of our popes have been targeted and attacked. During the tragic sack of Rome, on May 6, 1527, for example, 147 members of the Swiss Guards died while the other 42 were successful in saving Pope Clemens VII who made his way along a secret corridor to Castel Sant' Angelo. The life of the Pope was saved; however many Swiss guards lost their lives.

The popes have been targeted even in our contemporary world. It is important to study what prompted recent attacks on the popes and how the popes survived, and to see what we can learn from these attacks. In the first part of this chapter we provide the reader with facts about those attacks. We shall read about the three attacks directed against the persons of the Blessed Pope John Paul II, and the aggression done to Pope Benedict XVI. What we shall do in this section is just to inform our readers what happened, who did what, and what was done later. In the second part, we provide pastoral and theological reflections, and the spiritual insights in view of the attacks. With this portion of reflection, we seek to share with our readers a kind of a transformative impulse as regards the events that tested the security of the Roman Pontiffs. Let us now begin with the first attack levelled against Pope John Paul II.

Mehmet Ali Agca: Skilled Shooter who missed Target

The Blessed Pope John Paul II is remembered for many things he did for the Church during his long pontificate (1978-2005). Among all the others is that he is the Pope who endured sufferings. It ranges from the loss of his dear parents at his early age of life, his long fight with Parkinson's disease, and above all the assassination attempts against his life by a Turkish gunman and trained assassin.

On 16th October 1978 came the white smoke from the chimney of the Sistine Chapel. A total number of 111 Cardinals elected him at the age of 58. A few minutes afterwards Cardinal Felici announced solemnly from the balcony of St. Peter's Basilica that, "I announce to you a great joy; we have the Pope, whose name is Karol Wojytla." The new Pope hailed from East Europe. His native country Poland had been under the hegemony of the Russian Communist regime since after World War II. Under the control of the Kremlin, it was difficult to practice the Christian faith in public.

He was elected at a critical time. Speculations were mounting about what could have been the cause of the death of his predecessor the late Pope John Paul I, whose election after the death of Pope Paul VI, lasted only one month. The unexpected death fuelled a lot of speculation about the cause of death. An atmosphere of fear and uncertainty was reigning. The young Pope from Poland took office with courage assuring the Christian faithful all over the world, to have no fear to open the door wide for Christ. This words inspired many people who attended his inauguration Mass at St. Peter's Square.

Pope Johannes Paul II staunchly criticized the Soviet Union. While visiting his native country Poland in 1979, he strongly energized the people to feel proud of their Catholic faith. A huge crowd of people attended the Masses he celebrated, his homilies having a great impact on the Polish audience. The papal visit to Poland that year renewed the enthusiasm of the faith to the people of his native land. The first visit to Poland is described as "Nine Days that changed the World" in the film which is attributed to Newt Gingrich, a Republican in the US congress. The Soviet Union had intended to prevent the Pope from his mission but in vain (see Schönborn 2011:4). On 16th December 1980 the Pope wrote a very strongly worded letter to the General Secretary of the Communist Party Leonid Brezhnev in Moscow insisting on the right of the Polish people to practice the Christian faith. In addition, he compared the Soviet army to the Nazi soldiers.

This sounded a confrontational tone to the Kremlin, and Pope John Paul II was singled out as an enemy instead of being considered a partner for dialogue. It was a conspiracy between the Kremlin and the Bulgarian Security Service which facilitated the plot against the Pope (see Langford 2011). A man to accomplish this mission was a young Turkish Muslim who was 23 years of age. He was implicated in his home country of killing a journalist, and was recognized for his accurate shooting. It was easy to convince this man in payment to fulfil the mission to kill the Pope, because he belonged to a radical Islamic movement in his native country Turkey. Sophisticated plans were underway to eliminate the Polish Pope.

It was on the 13th May in 1981, the same day 64 years before that Madonna appeared to children at Fatima to bring them a message that the Holy Father will suffer a lot of pain. So it happened on that day around the afternoon hours: Pope John Paul II was driven in an open Papal mobile car around St. Peter's square, in order to greet pilgrims and those who sought a general audience with him. Mehmet Ali Agca had hidden himself among the crowd with a pistol Browning Parabellum 35. As the slow moving "Papal mobile" turned right at Peter's square at the end of Colonnade, Mehmet Ali pointed his pistol at the head of the Pope. Now he was at close range! A head shot at such range would make it impossible for the victim to survive. Suddenly, as Ali Agca finger pulled the trigger, the Pope had suddenly at the same time, bowed down because a young girl wanted the Pope to bless a painted portrait of a saint. In doing so, fortunately, the first shot missed the head of the Pope and shot the arm of a nun. He became nervous; he now no longer targeted the head of the Roman Pontiff, but shot at the stomach (see Englisch 2003:301). 'The bullet that cut through the pope's abdomen missed the main abdominal vein by five or six millimetres: Had that vital vein been severed, John Paul would have bled to death in five minutes' (Weigel 2010: 131). The police apprehended the assassin shortly after the shooting. During the interrogation, Mehmet Ali Agca did not reveal the motive why he targeted the Pope. Only later did the conspiracy of the Communist regime come to light through other sources such as authors, journalists and researchers (see Englisch 2003:301).

After the Pope was shot in the stomach, he was immediately rushed by Papal mobile through the streets of Rome to Gemelli clinic. Bleeding intensely, the Pope kept praying on the way "Maria, my mother...Jesus merciful" until he lost consciousness. At the clinic he received the anointing of the sick while placed under intensive care of the doctors. According to the account of Cardinal Stanislaw Dziwisz, at the hospital the Holy Father was in dire need of additional blood. The first transfusion was not successful because his body rejected the blood. The second transfusion attempt succeeded with blood from doctors themselves. The operation was successful, and the following day the Pope could receive Holy Communion from his private secretary Stanislaw Dziwisz. He pronounced his forgiveness to his assassin, telling those who were caring for him, "I pray for the brother who shot me, and forgive him."

The Pope spent three months at Gemelli clinic before he could resume office at the Vatican. This is how the Pontiff's life was saved. Many people have been asking, whether it was accidental that at the same time the fire was shot the young girl had asked the Pope to bless the photo image painting she had bought. Johannes Paul II himself believed that the attempt against his life was not accidental; it was linked with the prediction of Fatima. He was convinced that the Mother of God saved his life. It was for that, he set out for pilgrimage to Fatima on 13 May 1982 to thank the Mother of God.

Rebellious Priest who was intercepted

The Code of Canon law stipulates that a priest who makes an act of aggression against the person of the Holy Father commits a grave offense and risks dismissal from his priestly service. Despite the clear position of the Church, the Spanish priest attacked the Pope during his visit to Fatima. It was on this occasion Pope John Paul II thanked the Virgin Mary for protecting his life.

This event which had been kept secret for a long time has now been made known by the former secretary of the late Pope John Paul II in a film entitled "Testimony." The film narrates the life of Pope John Paul II, and is based on the memoirs of the Polish pope's secretary. It reveals the priest who came forward during the ceremony at the shrine in Fatima, and tried to assassinate the Pope with a bayonet. According to the Cardinal Dziwisz Archbishop of Cracow, the Holy Father was lightly wounded in 1982 by a knife attack by a deranged priest in Portugal. It was known that John Paul II was assaulted by a knife-wielding Spanish priest Juan Maria Fernandez Krohn, while visiting the shrine of Fatima in Portugal to give thanks for surviving an assassination attempt. He drew the blood of the Pope with the weapon.

But it was not known in 1982 that the Pope had been injured. "Today I can say what up to now we have kept a secret," Dziwisz said in the movie. "That priest wounded the Holy Father." The motive of the aggression by the ultraconservative priest was his opposition to the reforms adopted by the Catholic Church. Father Krohn was arrested by the police and served a sentence in a Portuguese prison before being expelled.

The release of this film which coincided with the elevation of the late Pontiff to the status of "Blessed" by Pope Benedict XVI on May 2011 provides testimony to this man of God. He had suffered much. In our contemporary culture which is a culture of death, John Paul II's life is a witness to life, a light shining in the darkness.

Susana Maiolo's Leap in St. Peter's Basilica

St. Peter's Basilica is fully packed during Christmas Eve Midnight Mass. People from all over the world come to Rome to celebrate with the Holy Father the nativity of the Lord. Many pilgrims seek to celebrate in a special way the whole Christmas Octave in the Eternal City that concludes with the Solemnity of Mary Mother of God on 1st January every year. The drama which took place on the Christmas Eve Midnight Mass, 24 December 2009, changed the atmosphere as the Pope was proceeding to the altar from the Sacristy to begin the Holy Mass.

Susanna Maiolo born in 1984, at the village of Frauenfeld (Switzerland), has a double citizenship; she is both Italian and Swiss. She jumped over a barrier and knocked Pope Benedict XVI down. In the commotion, the French cardinal Roger Etchegaray, too, fell to the ground, breaking his leg and hip. The reader can imagine the shock that gripped the Pope after being knocked down. The Christian faithful in Germany (the native country of the Benedict XVI) regard this special night as a night of quietness (*stille Nacht*), the time the world feels to have been blessed. It is indeed a holy night. It was difficult to imagine that the prince of evil was at work even on that night!

There is something we can learn from the reaction of the Pope during this event. Readers of this book should ask themselves for example, how do we react when we are knocked down unexpectedly in congested streets? Most of us are not patience; we panic and react with anger once attacked. This is quite different to how the Pope reacted to his aggressor. What is exceptional, and surely divine intervention played its part, the Pope at 82 years of age at the time of the event, was never injured and went to begin the Mass in a calm manner. This is exceptional. Perhaps what came into the mind of the Pope as he lay flat on the floor, are the words of Jesus spoken in a solemn way, "Very truly, I tell you, unless a grain of wheat falls into the earth…it remains just a single grain" (Jn 12:24).

What was astonishing was the attack was the second try by the same woman against the Roman Pontiff. Exactly a year earlier, Maiolo, wearing the same red hooded sweat shirt, also tried to reach the Pope during the Christmas Eve service, but was quietly escorted outside by security officers. Her repeated performance raised questions about the efficiency of the Vatican's security during public ceremonies. Some newspaper comments blamed the Vatican security system of inefficiency.

Authorities said that Maiolo is mentally disturbed and she was held for evaluation at a psychiatric hostel in Subiaco near Rome for one week (see *Wikipedia* 2011). Interrogated later by the Subiaco clinic staff, Susana Maiolo said she did not want to injure the Pope but wanted to ask him to help the poorest people in the world. The Pope's personal secretary Monsignor George Gaenswein, visited her at the clinic on 1 January 2010. He expressed the Pope's concern for her and said the Pope believed in her good intentions and had pardoned her.

It was informed later that the woman had an audience with the Pope from which she expressed her regret for attacking him and that she intended no harm whatsoever. The Holy Father also forgave the woman and wished her well with her health.

What Lessons Can We Draw from these Attacks?

The three attacks reflect the delicate situation of our time. On the one hand it challenges us to thinking about how we can provide security for the Pope. And on the other hand looking at the history of the papacy, we can be confidence that the protective hand of God is at work.

God is Our Refuge and Protector

Christians seek refuge in the Lord and trust in his care. Heavenly powers never sleep, and do not frustrate the Church. Despite the attacks, the lives of the Popes have been spared. In one event through the sacrifice of the Swiss Guards, and in others miraculously through divine interventions as we have seen with the release of Peter from prison and the protection of Pope John Paul II from the shooting by Mehmet Ali Agca. According to historian Lucetta Scaraffia, 'the evident intervention of a miraculous nature which caused the deflection of the shots fired by a very skilled killer just steps away from his target, and the subsequent saving of the Pope, have given this event a strong spiritual significance' (Scaraffia 2011). When one considers the deaths of several head of states targeted in human history around the world, despite their heavily guarded security system, and looking at the modesty security afforded to the Bishop of Rome, one cannot fail to discover the power of prayer and trust in God. We think here for example that, in 1962, the American president John Kennedy was targeted and was assassinated. At this time of insecurity we need to entirely trust in God. This is the first premise that we make as we conclude this chapter.

World Religions are still Violent

These aggressors have been from different backgrounds. Mehmet Ali Agca is a Turkish Muslim, by then a young man. The second aggressor Father Juan Maria Fernandez; is a Spanish Catholic priest, by then an advanced age adult person. The third attacker was a lay Catholic woman, of double nationalities, unmarried and in her middle age. From these three persons we can affirm that, evil is rampant throughout the world. Evil is neither respecter of gender nor specific religious backgrounds. One is not evil simply because he/she is a Christian or a Muslim. After September 11, for many people in the Western world, Islam was being perceived as a religion that sponsors violence and terrorism. Let us avoid stereotyping people.

The nature of attacks on popes shows that humans are prone to violence because the religion is made up of violent human beings. It is a shameful phenomenon found in World religions. Violence is common even among its clergy. Violence takes various forms: physical, sexual, and verbal aggression. 'There is a dark heart in every religion that nourishes contempt, persecution and crusade' (Baum 2005:91). All over the world, and especially in the West including the United States 'many people worship a God who supports violence, murder, and mayhem' (Crosby 2008:85). There are some pastors in the Evangelical movements who quite often refer to God who practices vengeance and punishment. Two examples can be picked here to illustrate this affirmation. When televangelist Pat Robertson declared that the stroke suffered by Ariel Sharon, former Prime Minister of Israel, was divine punishment for "dividing God's land" (see Crosby 2008:85). The second can be drawn from the statement made by mayor of Katrina-devastated New Orleans, affirming that the 'hurricanes that hit the nation in quick succession were a sign of God's anger towards the United States and toward black communities too, for violence and for fighting. "God is mad at America", he said' (Crosby 2008:85). Statements such as these, presents to the public a God who is crushing, and permits violence. This is contrary to the position of the Catholic Church.

One has to mention the *Reconstruction* branch of the Protestant mainline churches. This group feels they have been called to "reconstruct" the Christian community by converting to what the Bible teaches. Members of these movements based mainly in America think that; it is the moral responsibility of all Christians to recapture every institution for Jesus. Some Christians feel they have to do violence to convert everyone to Christ. One of those with this conviction was Paul Hill. He was inspired by the preaching of Michael Bray, a Lutheran pastor in Maryland. This pastor used biblical references and theological justification for warfare. In 1994, Hill killed a medical doctor who owned a clinic in Pensacola, Florida, where abortions were performed. He was killed along with his assistant (see Juergensmeyer 2008:185). There are numerous people who emphasize the *Reconstruction* and Christian Identity, justifying the murder of medical staff who practice abortions, gay married couples, lesbians, and transgendered individuals.

In Africa on March 17, 2000, an estimated 338 members of the *Movement for the Restoration of the Ten Commandments of God* died near the village of Kannungu in south western Uganda. Its church leaders, a man and a woman, claimed to receive regular visions from heaven. They told their followers that the coming of the Lord was very imminent. They mobilized them to assemble in the church building to pray and fast. The building was burned so that souls of the dead men and women should move quickly to heaven to meet God. As a result of this false eschatology many lives were lost (see Katongole 2005:119).

Televangelists like Harold Camping predicted that the world would end on 21 May 2011. First, he said, Rapture would come. This so called "Rapture" would occur on the given date above. On that day, Camping said, the good Christians-led, of course, by the faithful followers of his, were to be spirited into the air to meet the Lord Jesus Christ. He would catch them unto Himself and fly with them "home" to Heaven. Trumpets would sound the alarm to indicate the beginning of the end of the world. The end itself would occur on 21 October 2011 when the "sinners" or "unbelievers" left behind on the earth, would be struck by "Armageddon." That would mean the destruction of the earth. Due to this theory some people withdrew their money from the banks and spent it. Many people were overcome with fear, unsure of the disaster supposedly about to happen. As usual, again what was prophesied did not happen. Some people discovered it to be a lie and a trick. Some commentators questioned if the Rapture was to happen soon why Harold Camping was still soliciting donations on his website? (see *NewAfrican* 2011:77). Blessed John Paul II urges, 'Violence is a lie, for it goes against the truth of our faith, the truth of our humanity. Do not believe in violence. Do not support violence! It is not the Christian way. It is not the way of the Catholic Church. Believe in peace and forgiveness and love; for they are of Christ' (John Paul II, 1980). The whole reality unveils the complex nature of evil, and indeed the mystery of evil itself.

From these attacks one is again reminded of the need for interreligious dialogue. This is truly so because if a priest can attack the Pope, if a lay man can dare to attack a Pope, and a young Muslim believer can also harm the Pope, then religions are challenged from within by their own fundamentalist extremists, to invent relevant pastoral measures for mutual understanding. In the same way, the capacity of each religion to engage in self- criticism and correction is a compelling agenda not only for the religions but their neighbours, whose very life security may be put at risk.

Church as Suffering yet a Forgiving Community

The third premise is that the Church is a suffering community. There can be no Church of Christ without the cross. The two attacks on the two popes which took place in Rome were done in St. Peter's compound. One happened at the Square and the other one inside the Basilica. The city of Rome witnesses to this day the blood of martyrs of the Church. The attack by the priest took place outside the city of Rome, in Fatima. This place is related to the apparition of the Virgin Mary. The book of Revelation says:

A great portent appeared in the sun, with the moon under her feet, and on her head a crown of twelve stars. She was pregnant and was crying out in birth pangs, in the agony of giving birth. Then another portent appeared in heaven: a great red dragon, with seven heads and ten horns, and seven diadems on his heads...then the dragon stood before the woman who was about to bear a child, so that he might devour her child as soon as it was born...Then the dragon was angry with the woman, and went off to make war on the rest of her children, those who keep the commandments of God and hold the testimony" (Rev. 12:1-17).

The Virgin Mary protects the Church on her earthly pilgrimage. Concerning the secret of Fatima, Pope Benedict XVI says 'the Church continues to suffer... in every conceivable form, power threatens to trample down faith' (Benedict XVI 2005:151). The attack on the Pope at Fatima by a priest, just at the Marian shrine, makes real the messages of the famous "third secret of Fatima." This secret was not revealed until the Jubilee Year 2000 by Cardinal Joseph Ratzinger, at the behest of John Paul II. According to Pope Benedict XVI, 'the message is not a thing of the past...The Church continues to suffer, and a threat still hangs over man...Even now there is tribulation. Even now, in every conceivable form, power threatens to trample down faith' (Benedict XVI 2005:151).

The Church suffers much in every age. Yet it pronounces forgiveness and prays for the forgiveness of sins of everyone. This was especially true in the Jubilee Year 2000, when Pope John Paul II prayed for the forgiveness of sins committed in the name of the Church, and those who have persecuted the Church all these years. Steps taken by the popes after attacks to meet those who attacked them and pronounce reconciliation are exemplar.

Let us take a look to see the implication of these steps. The decision of Pope John Paul II to go to prison by his own free will, to be "enclosed for a while inside the bars" is a worthy act. It shows a spirit of humility that is to be emulated. For many people, the prison is a place for "bad guys," and "condemned people." The Holy Father neither waited nor ordered his convicted attacker to come to his palace, rather he lowered himself and followed Mehmet Ali to his place of confinement. He wanted to tell the world that a prison is place for human beings. Prisoners are persons like everyone else called to become more human every day. The inmates are challenged in correctional centres to transform. The Pope visiting Ali Agca in his prison cell conveys a message that even an enemy needs to be approached with love and humility, for we are all part of the *humus* made of dust. From the Book of Genesis, we read that God made a human being from the soil. We are all soiled. We have to go to the places where the jobless, homeless, the condemned, and all those abandoned by the wrath of society. In doing so, we can allow new life to begin in others. We can serve these people better by soiling our hands and our bodies too. A prison, like any human institution is a pastoral area of the Church, a place where reconciliation can also take place.

Now let us move to Pope Benedict XVI. After being attacked in the Basilica, he allowed an audience with Susana Maiolo. The Pope knew that the woman was mentally disturbed, but acting in *persona Christi*; he wanted to see her in person. The Holy Father thought it an opportune time to talk to her and express his solidarity with her. In their meeting, reconciliation was made possible. Susana Maiolo felt herself blessed to have met with the Holy Father. This act shows how the Church cares for every human person no matter what their issues may be.

"Woe" Are the Peace Makers

The fourth premise we make is that "if you want to stand for peace prepare to sacrifice your life!" According to the beatitudes pronounced by Jesus Christ at the sermon on the mount, peace makers called the *makarios*, the blessed for they shall inherit the land. The compliment of Jesus to the peace makers resides in the fact that in dispensing reconciliation and harmony among nations these distinguished people do what the Prince of Peace himself did. They are a people who wish goodness in other human beings, and the whole creation. But in doing so, they have to pay a price. They are drawn very closely to the Mother Earth (the dust) and also to the cross of Jesus.

Mahtama Gandhi, for instance offered his life for the cause of the poor and peace. His bold dedication to the cause of peace and justice resulted in his arrests. 'He was arrested twelve times and spent almost six years behind bars (2,089 days in Indian prisons and 249 days in South African prisons). Jail did not diminish his vision, and in many ways it deepened his trust in God' (Groody 2007:157).

Another important personality to be mentioned is John F. Kennedy, the former President of the United States. Deeply rooted in the values of his Democratic Party and as Catholic, the President pursued the cause of non violence in U.S international politics. 'When everyone else had signed off on an invasion of Cuba, he would not give the go-ahead to an impatient military and thus avoided World War III' (Greeley 2007:2). It was his pacifistic approach that did not give room for America to show forth its military superiority to the world, a gesture which angered some conservative Americans. As a result he was killed. He paid the price for his love to the poor and his dedication for peace.

There are many people who have lost their lives in their struggle for peace. The Brazilian Sergio Vieira de Mello the UN envoy in conflict resolution resolutions was described by UN analyst as "the most experienced crisis manager in the U.N. and perhaps its single most gifted official" (Hanson 2011:221). Just as he had successfully accomplished overseeing East Timor's transition to independence, the former U.N Secretary General Kofi Annan sent him to Baghdad as UN special representative there. While there he worked round the clock and refused tight security measures and bodyguard convoys around him. On August, 2003 he was killed by insurgents who bombed the Canal Hotel where he was living. Peacemaking and peacekeeping have become very dangerous in this world that is obsessed with the show of military prowess (see Hanson 2011:221).

Tragedies facing peacemakers baffle us. Why do peacemakers become targets? Why should popes like Blessed John Paul II and Benedict XVI be targets of assassination attempts? We forget that Jesus Christ and John the Baptist who followed the way of non violence were killed though they were innocent. Jesus was Jewish patriot, but arousing his Palestinian people to throw off the Roman yoke was not part of his message. Neither did John the Baptist. It was a cruel paradox that two men who preached peace and submission to the will of God, should be put to death on charges quite contrary to what they stood for (Sloyan 2008:23).

People who passed judgment to eliminate Jesus Christ such as Pilate and Herod were hungry of power. Both the Roman lawyer and the Jewish king were construed by the evangelist to be cowardly dishonest. Mark reports the beheading of John the Baptist. The assassination of John the Baptist teaches that people like Herod are obsessed with power and have neither interest in defending justice nor in standing up for the rights of innocent people. Pilate and Herod, though different in career and nationalities, are similar in that all they want is to conserve their power and status.

Like Jesus Christ and John the Baptist, our popes will continue to be targeted as long as they stand to defend the truth and fight for justice and peace. The *motto* inscribed on the coat- of- arms of Pope Pius XII was "peace is the work of justice." As Vicar of Christ on earth, the Pope strives to point out to Christians and the world, the right path for humanity. The Book of the Acts of the Apostles often describes the Christian faith as "the way" (see Acts 9:2; 18:25-26; 19:9, 23; 24:14, 22). Consequently, discipleship involves following the master in the way of truth and in suffering to defend the truth even to the point of death. This is rightly so because, "truth begets hatred." And in the society we live in people, are good at relativism, denying the truth as it is. The world as we experience it 'is profoundly irrational. Things do not always make sense, and if we are going to be honest, we must admit that very often we have no explanation for things we experience, like massacres, torture, the sexual abuse of small children, and the maiming of innocent people-to name but a few' (Nolan 2009:24).

The Pope as a messenger of peace and as one, who stands for justice in the world, is likely always to come into conflict with the secular powers of the world. The nation states and multinational companies work on the logics of power and keeping status quo. 'The coercive power of the empire, the power of wealth, or just simply, power, becomes envisioned as the most "effective" means' (Camp 2008:36). These powers will not tolerate anyone who preaches against the manifestation of their power and interest. Not even the Pope. Opposing strongly the American pre-emptive war in Iraq, "War" the Pope said on Jan. 13, 2003, "cannot be decided upon, even when it is a matter of ensuring common good, except as the very last option and in accordance with very strict conditions, without ignoring the consequences from the civilian population both during and after military operations." Pope John Paul II heard many voices in America which criticized him. The *Wall Street Journal* had reprimanded the Pope for intervening in the "war on terrorism" (see Greeley 2007:60). Andrew Greeley, a Catholic priest, and one of the most influential Catholic scholars in America was outspoken against the Iraq War in a series of his articles. He received hate mail for his opposition against the Iraq War which he describes as an "unjust, stupid and criminal war." He writes:

I get a lot of hate mail from conservative Catholics who are furious at my criticism of the Iraq war. You have no right to use your office, I am told, to criticize our fine Christian president. You are a disgrace to the priesthood. I may leave the Catholic Church because of you. Why don't you quit the priesthood now and stop harming the Church? You are even worse than the priests who abuse little boys (Greeley 2007:111)

This confirms that the witness for justice and peace is a way of martyrdom. Those who oppose the use of violence and war are in turn targeted and crushed by the forces of evil. Albert Nolan is right when he opines that, '...and while in a sense money rules the world, as it has done for thousands of years, the really oppressive power in the human world is the gun' (Nolan 2006:31). As Joseph Pierre Belloc, the Anglo-French writer asserted a century ago "whatever happens, we have the Maxim gun and they have not." Therefore 'mighty is right.' The Pope ought to keep quite if he wants a world security.

Let Us Care the People with Down syndrome

Now let us make the last premise as we come to conclude this chapter. "Let us welcome people with down syndrome." This is what we have learned from the hospitality of Pope Benedict XVI when he had an audience with Susan Maiolo. It is necessary to know that people with physical, psychological, and mental problems have an inner cry of being neglected. Children born with Down syndrome encounter unwelcome atmosphere in some families. They are locked and hidden in rooms when visitors come. In many occasions they are denied the joy of community unlike the children without mental and physical problem. In family homes persons with disabilities are served food separately in some places. Facing discrimination in their own families, they grow up feeling as if they are "useless" members of society. This results in perpetual depression which can precipitate a rage likely to burst out at places where the love of the neighbour is preached as empty rhetorical eloquence. 'The mystery of people with disabilities is that they long for authentic and loving relationships more than for power. They are not obsessed with being well-suited in a group that offers acclaim and promotion. They are crying for what matters most: love' (Hauerwas: Vanier 2008:30).

The fact that the same woman tried to reach the Pope at Easter vigil Mass 2008, only to be intercepted by the security guide may motivate more interest as what was behind her move. She wanted to have an opportunity to meet and talk with the Pope. Many people who suffer the Down syndrome do not have friends. 'The problem was not that they lived alone but they lacked a network of friends. We have to discover more fully that the church is a place of compassion and fecundity, a place of welcome and friendship. We need time to listen and to understand people with communications problems. It takes time to become a friend of people with disabilities' (Hauerwas: Vanier 2008:37).

The attempt which Susana Maiolo made to approach the Pope before she was controlled by the security officers at Christmas 2008 could have aroused a pastoral search among Vatican officials to seek an opportunity to talk with this young woman, listen to her personal stories and discover what was behind the decision she made. One can imagine how delighted she was, when Monsignor Georg Gaenswein visited her at the clinic where she was treated after assaulting the Pope in 2009. The happiest moment for this young lady came when she was accompanied by two of her family members for a brief audience with Pope Benedict after the morning general audience on 13 January 2010 in a room adjoining the Pope Paul VI Audience Hall. Maiolo told the Pope she regretted the incident. A face to face encounter between people with disabilities and prelates in the Church is preferable. Disabled people yearn strongly for the pastoral touch from priests and bishops. Generally, people with disabilities are placed in special centres. In their situation of being "caged" away from those who are mentally normal, 'the story begins with a huge gap of injustice and pain. It is a gap between the so-called "normal" world and the people who have been pushed aside, put into institutions, excluded from our societies because they are weak and vulnerable' (Hauerwas: Vanier 2008:29).

The attack of the Pope by a woman with mental problem, should guide us to take care of people with disabilities. Certainly, the Church is assisting these people in special centres where religious sisters and other lay workers attend and assist them to recuperate. Those with Down syndrome and other mental and emotional disorders are 'living icons of the crucified Son" (Hauerwas: Vanier 2008:39). They can help us 'if we welcome them. They can lead us progressively out of the world of competition and the need to do great things towards a world of communion of hearts, a life that is simple and joyful where we do small things with love' (Hauerwas: Vanier 2008:40). The pastoral care for handicapped people should be intensified. People with extreme depression, including those suffering Down syndrome often time commit suicide, and in some cases turn wild targeting people they think are a cause of their plight. Some of these people consider themselves to have no meaning at all! They simply regard themselves not to matter at all. With such depression the temptation may be to try to do something that will make them known and publicized. One of the likely options could be that of assassinating a very important person.

The attack by Susana Maiolo's on 24th December 2009, unveils the need to engage people with disabilities. This is important in the situation of violence today. The handicapped and all those who suffer disabilities of any sort want to feel the warmth and care from their brothers and sisters who are in good health. They expect much from priests and bishops too as pastors of the soul. Once such people are not cared for they may resort to violence and target pastors. It is important to let them feel in community. 'There are three activities that are absolutely vital in the creation of community. The first is eating together around the same table. The second is praying together. And the third is celebrating together' (Hauerwas: Vanier 2008:37). Pope John Paul II at Christmas used to organize a meal together with jobless and disabled people in the city of Rome. Initiatives like this are very significant today when many people are depressed. Lack of engagement, lack of love to the people with disabilities may prompt them to turn aggressive and dangerous for the security of the clergy.

We must say that the community of faith in its entirety has to take care of people with disabilities. The Church is admonished in the Pauline literary corpus as well as the pastoral letters to assist in a particular way the weakest members of society. It is in this light that the former Archbishop of Los Angeles (U.S.A) Cardinal Roger Mahony, in one of his pastoral letters to the Archdiocese entitled, *Creating Culture of Life* underlines that "Any society, any nation, is judged on the basis of how it treats its weakest members...the last, the least, the littlest."

To conclude this chapter let us state that, attacks on popes as narrated in the passages above, should rally the Catholic faithful to be watchful all the time. From the family to parish communities the security of every member is a responsibility of all. It is important to care for everyone and keep everyone who takes part in the liturgy assured of his/her security. Members of the community with disabilities for example, should be taken care in a responsible manner and with joy. This is important so they feel that they matter in life, loved and prized by God and those around them. During the worship services, at the Holy Mass and adoration services, any suspicious movements of people should be politely intercepted before any harm is done. The protection of the pastors depends on the watchful eyes of the congregation at large. The lives of the pastors are important for the community of the faith, so is the life of everyone. Every life is sacred and should be protected.

4

Like a lamb led to the Slaughter

Prophet Isaiah in one of the songs of the suffering servant depicts the servant of God as one who is humiliated and accepts affliction which he suffers with exceptional docility. The meekness and the complete innocence of the servant of God in the face of the injustices he endures in tranquillity leads prophet Isaiah to describe the servant of God as a lamb. "He was oppressed, and he was afflicted, yet he did not open his mouth: like a lamb that is led to the slaughter" (Is. 53:7).

The Pope is addressed with different titles, one of which is the "servant of the servants of God." This title originates from Pope Gregory the Great (590-610) who was a Benedictine monk. The rule of St. Benedict for his monks encourages in a special way the virtue of humility. The title "servant of the servants of God" matches very well with the image of the Lamb. This image as applied to Jesus Christ appears in the New Testament, especially in the book of Revelation. The book uses apocalyptic language with warlike images that may seem to encourage violence. The image of the Lamb as referred to Jesus in the book, interestingly, offers a contrary vision. The Lamb is hunted to be devoured by the beast (see Rev. 17:14). This lamb is spoken as worthy to be slaughtered (see Rev. 5:12), and by the shedding of its blood is designated to shepherd many nations (see Rev. 14:4). Such an image brings forth the picture of the suffering servant. Jesus conquers the evil of the dragon through 'reverse fighting, by accepting suffering rather by causing others to suffer' (Garrity Ranaghan 2011:67). In the era of rebellion and violence such as we have today the Bishop of Rome preaches the reverse of violence, pursuing the way of the innocent lamb.

John Paul II and Benedict XVI are the closest Popes we know. The late Pope John Paul II gave to Christianity a positive look at the cross. His long illness and a prolonged pontificate gave the world hope amidst suffering. He would always greet the crowd while holding his cross firmly. The power of the cross energized him to endure tribulations. At his first meeting with young people all over the world in Rome in 1984, he entrusted to them the colossal wooden crucifix, which is now known as the *World Youth Day Cross*, to be carried throughout the world as an all-time symbol of the love of Christ for humanity.

Pope Benedict has crafted his pontificate to the image of the Good Shepherd. And let us not forget, the good shepherd lays down his life for the sheep (see Jon 10:11). Benedict XVI is the first Pope in our modern era to design his coat of arms without the tiara (which symbolized the secular power of the Pope), replacing it with a simple Bishop's mitre. In addition to that, for the first time a pallium (stole worn by metropolitan bishops) is included in the papal coat of arms. In relation to that, Pope Benedict XVI is seen in many stadia and open places where he celebrates Mass with his pastoral staff. This is made in a traditional shape as those used by Popes in the early centuries of Christianity. This shows that the papacy is to serve ecumenical endeavours. This is especially clear when one finds that the crucifix in the pontifical staff has no image of the crucified as was the case with his predecessor. It is a pastoral gesture which is presumably pleasing to Protestant churches.

Television channels diffuse the images of the Pope all over the world. The idea of the Pope as "global cross carrier" and "pallium bearer" emerges, thus raising a concern for his security. Let us begin to look at the Pope as a cross bearer around the globe but who is not crusader.

The Cross Bearer who is not Crusader

As pastor of global Catholicism Pope Benedict XVI carries his pastoral stock painted in bronze with the cross at the top of it. The Pope draws huge crowds in every diocese he visits in the world. The people who attend papal open air Masses are from all religious backgrounds. By virtue of his high office as successor of Peter, he has virtually an overwhelming influence on Christianity's relationship with the other religions of the world (see Allen, Jr 2004:20).

Contemporary Hostility against Crucifixes

As the global cross bearer, the Pope encounters the world that is rebellious to the "Gospel of Suffering" preached by the cross. The cross bearer around the globe has the possibility of being ridiculed and even targeted for presenting the symbol which identified with Christianity. Starting with his native continent Europe, which is described by some scholars, as "a Godless Europe" (Jenkins 2007:9), it is now 'the most secular continent on the earth' (Jenkins 2007:1). Due to the presence of many immigrants from Eastern Europe, and particularly those of Turkish origin, some observers see 'Europe making a wholesale transition into Muslim world, becoming part of Eurabia' (Jenkins 2007:4). The general trend in Western Europe lacks commitment to faith and family, has evaporating moral standards and plummeting birth rates, creating a society that is literally unsustainable (see Jenkins 2007:9).

The Pope carries the cross around the globe. He is aware of the new trend which opposes the display of crucifixes in public places. Recently the bishops of Switzerland issued a statement denouncing the Swiss governments' hostility to the display of Christian symbols in public (see Nick 2010). In fact the Swiss bishops are experiencing an anti-Christian mentality that is breaking out in different places in Europe. In Italy, Switzerland, Austria, France and Germany parents are opposed to their children to studying in schools which have crucifixes hanging in the classrooms. They say that this is discriminatory to non-Christians. Some feel that the practice of putting crucifixes in classrooms, dining rooms, halls and offices, imply that the Italian State for example, promotes the Catholic Church and Christianity in State owned schools which are supposed to be secular. The opposition to the display of Christian symbols in public tends to hide a particular hostility towards Christianity under the guise of tolerance towards other faiths. The Swiss bishops speak of 'strong hostility that is manifested against religious symbols in public place' (Nick 2010). There is danger of destroying the Christian foundation which has been established in Europe for centuries. The paradox here is that while there seems to be strict regulation as regards the display of religious symbols in public, a footballer wearing a cross, making a sign of the cross and kneeling down to pray on the pitch will go unnoticed and yet a nurse, doctor or teacher risks facing disciplinary action for donning a crucifix while on duty.

One of the salient signs of hostility displaying of crucifixes in public places is the judicial appeal taken by an Italian woman against the government. In *Lautsi v. Italy*, an atheistic mother of two public school children challenged the Italian policy allowing crucifixes in public schools. After losing in the Italian court, she appealed to the European Court of Human Rights, arguing that the presence of these crucifixes in public schools violated her and her children's right to religious freedom and to a secular education guaranteed by the European convention on Human Rights. On Nov.3, 2009, a unanimous seven-judge chamber of the European Court held for Ms. Lautsi. On March 18, the Grand Chamber reversed and held 15-2 ruled in favour of Italy (see Witte Jr 2011). Despite this verdict the European nations remain widely divided on whether and where to display various religious symbols (see Witte Jr 2011). The situation is precarious and hostility towards the cross in public is an actuality.

The prohibition of religious symbols in public places has its paradox. In the field of sports, for example, there is much more toleration. One wonders if people who advocate the removal of crucifixes are not aware that Jesus was crucified on the hill top and displayed for his enemies to see and mock him. All in all, it is to be stated that contemporary European societies face real dangers, demanding innovative and imaginative approaches that challenge European values. Moreover, governments are handicapped by a pervasive secularism that finds it difficult to treat seriously religious concerns, motivations, or sensitivities (see Jenkins 2007:24-25).

This mounting hatred by radical groups against those who publicly witnesses their faith convictions, provide a ground for concern for the security of the Pope. The Pope preaches the Christ crucified, in the word of St. Paul, " For Jews demand signs and Greeks desire wisdom, but we proclaim Christ crucified, a stumbling block to Jews and foolishness to Gentiles, but to those who are called, both Jews and Greeks, Christ is the power and wisdom of God" (1 Cor 1:21-25). The Pope carries the cross, not as an instrument of coercion on others but as an expression of faith. 'Followers of Christ must be willing to follow him to the cross, to be crucified with him. We exist as a "cruciform church," as a community shaped like the cross' (Camp 2008:120). It is a cruciform Church, which is transformed to become a cross-shaped people in a secular world. The Pope carries the cross, and tells the world on behalf of all Christians, "we are afflicted in every way, but not crushed; perplexed, but not driven to despair; persecuted, but not forsaken; struck down, but not destroyed; always carrying in the body the death of Jesus, so that the life of Jesus may be visible in our bodies" (2 Cor 4:8-9).

Mistaken Idea that the Pope is Chief Crusader

Some radical Muslims consider the Pope as "Chief Crusader" who hates Islam and strongly opposes the spread of Islam. Mistaken view tries to convince Muslims that the Pope is an enemy of Islam, whose only agenda is the prosperity of Christianity. The use of the word "crusade" as pronounced by an American president gave the message that the war against terrorism was a crusading mission. According to Andrew Greeley, 'the president's ...invitation to all nations, including the Islamic ones, to join our crusade against terrorism boggles the mind. It is like asking Jews to join pogrom. Not to realize that the word "crusade" means to Muslims is an intolerable display of superficiality' (Greeley 2007:5). The language of "crusade" repeated several times during the War in Iraq and Afghanistan, in fact sparked sentiment of anger among Muslim extremists everywhere, threatening the *Jihad* war against the West.

The idea of the "crusade war" can be allowed to grow in the minds of Muslims albeit ignorantly, by the presence of Church ministers who offer spiritual services to members of the allied forces during their operations in a predominantly Muslim countries. The American, Great Britain, French, Italian, Spanish, and Australian combat troops are assisted spiritually by army chaplains (ordained priests) to ensure that military personnel have access to the Holy masses and regularly receive sacraments. The presence of the Church personnel in the context of "military" operations may mistakenly convey the idea that the Church is part of the mission. This idea may be allowed to flow especially when the allied forces offer protection to foreign volunteers some of them spearheading an aggressive form of evangelism. Borderless missionary activities in places like Afghanistan and Iraq are executed with the thinking that Christians have a duty to convert Muslims as part of their mandate to fight evil spirits and heal the world. One has to recall that on September 14, 2001, President George W. Bush declared in the National Cathedral in Washington, D.C., that the task of America was to rid the world of evil. It is easy to confuse such missionary ambitions as receiving the support of the state. On July 19, 2007 in Afghanistan, the Taliban militia kidnapped 23 South Korean Presbyterian Church Christians. The motive behind the abduction is said that to be 'Korean churches' overzealous mission activities as well as irresponsible mission methods and strategies that are inconsiderate and insensitive to other cultures' (Kim 2010:4). After the event debates in media, and public forums in South Korea accused the South Korean government for accepting to become an ally to the Americans to send troops in Afghanistan. To this point, it is necessary to know that a proselytising missionary zeal is not supported by the Roman Catholic Church. In all these circumstances, since the Pope is considered as the virtual leader of World Christianity, there is a temptation to look at him as a "chief crusader."

Thinking that the Pope is a Crusader is a mistaken position. It shows that the most radical parts of Islam and the extremists have not understood the papacy and what it is about. We begin with the cross; the Pope carries the cross as the Vicar of Christ. For Christians 'the cross contains the message that God himself is someone who suffers, that through suffering he is fond of us, that he loves us' (Benedict XVI 2010:62). The cross is a sign of love and appeals for forgiveness. It is not an instrument for proselytizing. The Pope while carrying the cross all over the world shows his solidarity with people of all walks of life. The cross is a symbol of humility. As cross bearer the Bishop of Rome makes any visit as one who is ready to share with the people who suffer infirmities. He is scheduled to visit the sick in hospitals and prisoners in correctional centres. He extends hands to leaders of World Religions and makes dialogue with them. Moreover, the Pope struggles for the right of Christians to express religious witness publicly as he fights for the rights of Muslims and members of other religions to do the same.

Christians are tolerant, and in that respect allow others to have their self-image. We are grateful that in the countries along the Persian Gulf (Qatar, Abu Dhabi, Dubai, Kuwait) there are churches in which Christians can worship, and we wish it to be like this everywhere. For this reason it goes without saying that Muslims in our countries can also gather in mosques for prayer. As for burqa, I see no reason for a general ban. Some say that many women would not wear the burqa voluntarily at all and that it is actually a violation of women. One can of course, not agree to that. But if they want to wear it voluntarily, I do not know why it must be prohibited (Benedict XVI 2010:62).

We find that regarding the Pope as a crusader carrying the cross around the globe misses the point again for the simple reason that the popes of recent times have strongly opposed the use of violence. They have advocated the "culture of peace."

The starting point for these novel reflections in the Catholic Church is Pope John XXIII's release of the encyclical *Pacem in terris* (1963), which called for a new approach to the pursuit of peace. The Church is determined to promote the culture of peace. She has moved away from accepting war in some circumstances, the so called "Just war" theory which was supported by Christian thinkers such as St. Augustine and St. Thomas Aquinas from the past. In those days, the empires and chiefdoms were struggling to expand; different religions and denominations were competing to proselytize new converts and territories. Conflicts and wars were used on many occasions to reach a desired goal. In such circumstances the "just war theory" applied to plead for princes to resort to ethical engagement, before they took decisions to go to the battlefield which involved soldier to soldier combats.

Nowadays however with sophisticated weapons of mass destruction such as nuclear bombs, cluster bombs etc, there is in principle no just war in which only combatants are exclusively killed. Usually innocent people are quite often victims. Vatican Council II and recent popes have adopted a pacifist position. Their teachings to be realistic were not intended to forbid the people to defend themselves against an attack by an external aggressor. 'The Church honours the pacifist decision of conscientious objectors and urges the intention of non-violent strategies for the resolution of grave conflicts, but it does not abrogate the legitimacy of self-defense' (Baum 2005:84). During the discussion on war and peace at Vatican Council II, several bishops, invoking the witness of Franz Jaegerstätter, demanded that the Church change its teaching and honour the conscience of Catholic who refuses to bear arms, the new teaching is endorsed in *Gaudium et spes* (* 78).

The clear position of the Roman Catholic Church against warfare was echoed strongly during the October 1965 General Assembly of the United Nations. On this occasion Pope Paul VI inspired by the mind of Vatican Council II told the assembly, please "Never War again." To open a stage for the "culture of peace" Pope Paul VI instituted the World Peace Day, which has been celebrated with special prayers every January 1, beginning in 1968, on which occasion the Pope offers a message in support of peaceful co-existence and universal solidarity (see Baum 2005:88).

The position against the use of violence as a means of solving problems is in compromise to the "culture of peace" which the Church seeks to safeguard. It is in this vision that Pope John Paul II disapproved the Gulf War in 1993, the bombing of Afghanistan after the terror attack on September 11, 2001 and the war against Iraq designed to oust President Sadam Hussein in 2003.

A changed attitude of the Church since the end of Vatican II (1962-1965), acknowledges the values found in other world religions. This is a new ethical principle (see Baum 2005:89). In the past, 'the Church has never applied this principle in its relation to other religious communities, nor in its response to its own internal conflicts' (Baum 2005:89). This recognition of values which are inherent in other faith backgrounds is a hallmark for the "culture of peace." In a widely read book, *The Clash of Civilizations and the Remaking of the World Order* (1996), Samuel Huntington has argued that the world religions have incompatible values, the civilizations they have created will inevitably clash (see Baum 2005:95). The book apparently warns of the threatening clash between the Muslim world and the West.

However, both John Paul II and Benedict XVI are of the opinion that world religions have many values in common and that their destiny is to co-operate and together protect the well-being of humanity and the earth. The position of the Church is geared to promote dialogue through mutual listening, reconciliation, the pursuit of human freedom and dignity as the right way to attain harmony. Indeed, we still have a long way to go. The Muslim and Hindu brothers and sisters may still have feelings of mistrust and hold grudges against the Church. It is important to know that, the very idea of the *culture of peace* is new in the Catholic tradition. Centuries ago, 'we did not engage in dialogue with people and communities that disagreed with us; we did not make an effort to look upon their ideas and practices from their point of view; we did not think that careful listening to the other was our moral duty; we reacted to dissenters in our midst and followers of other religions in a defensive manner' (Baum 2005:98).

Considering the Pope as "chief crusader" is incorrect given the way the Pope describes himself when he visits the people of different cultures. In the past popes have preferred to identify themselves as "missionaries." But in the contemporary era the popes travel across borders as "pilgrims." This is very significant. In the present context the word "mission" is viewed by some in a negative way. Some think that the concept still harbours imperialistic attitudes of the colonial era. Now in some parts of the world, expatriate missionaries are looked upon with suspicion and are seen as people who seek to proselytize and spread their own culture. This is obvious in the way some languages in global South define westerners. In Kiswahili for example, the language which is widely spoken in East and some parts of central Africa, the white person is called *mzungu*. This concept has two connotations from its semantics. In the first place the vocabulary *mzungu* stems from the root *–zunguk-* which forms the verb *kuzunguka* (to go around). A white person is someone who moves around the globe to see everything that is there and impose Western values as he/she thinks *prima facie* that Western values are universally applicable. This position stresses the understanding that the white person is someone who is passionate with imperialistic and touristic interests. The second meaning of the word *mzungu* stems from the Kiswahili noun *mizungu* which means "strange knowledge," or mysteries. In this sense the white person is understood as someone who has access to strange knowledge, to the mysteries of the unknown God. He/she is a person who has brought to the Africans the "strange" God with its strange cultures. This second meaning implies that the white person has proselytizing attitudes.

Thus, terminologies like *mission, mzungu, blacks* and many words like these are transferred from the past to the next generations unfortunately with their colonial touch fuelling the mistrust of the other. Hence the shift of the Pope's self description from being a "missionary" to "pilgrim" is very significant in so far as the sentiments of members of other World religions are concerned. There was an incident briefly recorded by Lucien Legrand, a biblical scholar who worked in India for long time. He refers to the use of the notion of "mission" or "missionary" by two different popes, Paul VI and John Paul II. Legrand relates that when Pope Paul VI visited India, his remarks did not find a welcome in Mumbai (Bombay) when in a public address he described his visit to the sub-continent as a "missionary" journey. In contrast, Pope John Paul II, raised no such hostility at all several years later when he referred to his own visit to India as a "pilgrimage."

To be sure, Pope Paul VI's choice of the word "missionary" may have been unfortunate in these circumstances, uttered in a land so very dominated by non-Christian religions and faith. This self-designation suggested that he was not about the business of converting the predominantly Hindu nation to Catholicism (see Magesa 2006:16). Secondly, the notion of "pilgrimage," as used by Pope John Paul II was certainly prudent in these circumstances. It implied that he 'was a learner in India, and was not about the business of imposing his Christian faith on anyone. The notion also conveyed a ring of respect for India's religious and cultural patrimony' (Magesa 2006:16).

The word *pilgrim* has its origin from two Latin words (*per* – through + *ager* – field, country, or land), which means one that comes from foreign parts, a stranger, one on a journey, a wayfarer, a sojourner to a foreign land who counts on the hosts to share with him something substantial. Being a pilgrim is neither an accident, nor a downgrade instead it is the way the Christians look upon themselves. It is their status of humility and hope. It is the identity of the Israelites as they confess their status of "being strangers and pilgrims in this land" (Heb 11:13). The Christians as members of the new Israel, (the Church) are very much conscious of their status as being *pilgrims*. The Pope tells the Indians that he visits them as "a pilgrim" sound to the ears of Hindus that the distinguished guest from Rome comes to learn something there and his approach rings the tone that God had already set his foot on their soil there before the Pope arrived.

The Bishop of Rome addressing himself as "pilgrim" tells the assembly he meets overseas that he is a sojourner. He comes as a guest, not as the owner of the house (see Lk 10:1-6). In this identity the leader of the Catholic Church accepts the marginalization which the Church suffers in different parts of the world without losing love. The post- Christendom era provides a clear reality that Christians are never truly at home in the world. As pastor, the Pope teaches the Catholic faithful to learn to become strangers even within their native localities. This is important for a spirituality which is adapted to welcome "strangers." The host communities must overcome the pride of self- confidence and self-enclosure. As partakers of Holy Communion, the *Viaticum* which is the food of seafarers, (travellers) we find that the migrants and strangers among us are not "the others" but are fellow strangers. At the Holy Eucharist it is God who is the provider to us all. It is God who is the Home-maker, and the migrants are partners with us. This truth can be noticed during papal visits. Even the Pope is a pilgrim, a visitor and a guest, and a Vicar of Christ on Earth. He represents the one who makes us at home. For that the Pope is at the same time a "local pastor" who carries the pallium everywhere. When he visits dioceses all over the world, the local archbishops do not wear the pallium. It is the Pope who does that as Vicar of Christ.

The *Pallium* shouldered Pontiff across Boarders

The pallium is an ordinary insignia of patriarchs, and archbishops in their metropolitan sees which they can wear also when they visit the suffragan dioceses under their metropolitan. It is only the Pope and because of his capacity as the universal Pastor of the universal Church, who can wear the pallium everywhere in the world. This distinguishes the Pope as a possible target of martyrdom globally in so far as the pallium is concerned.

Like a Slaughtered Lamb

Let us look at what the pallium is made of and get hold of its meaning and the implication it has to those who wear it. It is woven of pure wool. The wool is taken from lambs blessed at the memorial of St. Agnes, which is celebrated in the Roman Catholic Church liturgical calendar on 21st January. The name of this saint *Agnes* comes from the Latin word, *Agnus* which means the lamb. Agnes is revered as the patron saint of the City of Rome. The young virgin lady was martyred in the ancient Rome by Emperor Diocletian (284-305 AD). During the memorial day of the saint, the General Abbot of the Lateran Basilica choir, the community of which is entrusted to St. Agnes, celebrates a high Mass in the Basilica. At the end of the Mass which is usually well attended by devoted Catholics mainly from the Archdiocese of Rome, the Abbot receives two lambs from the Trappist monks of the Tre Fontane Abbey, decorated with flowers and, placed on the altar. The lambs "innocent ones" are a symbol of Christ-who is the Lamb of God. The two lambs on this day represent St. Agnes. She was killed innocently offering herself to be murdered for preserving her chastity. Church artists have portrayed her with an image of a lamb. The General Abbot blesses the lambs with these words, "Almighty God, let your blessings come upon these lambs from which its wool the pallium for the Pope, patriarchs and archbishops will be made" (see Hubert 2001:178) After this rite in the Lateran Basilica, the lambs are sent to the Vatican where they are handed to the Holy Father in a solemn rite. The Pope blesses the lambs and hands them over to the Benedictine Sisters of Santa Cecilia in Trastevere. It is in this convent where wool from the lambs is taken to make the pallium (see Hubert 2001:179).

The wearing of the pallium by the Pope and archbishops has a long history. The Bishops of Rome have worn it since the fourth century of Christianity. The shoulder is used in many cultures by men to carry heavy loads. Placing the pallium on the shoulder of the prelate, intends to present the message that the Pope, the patriarchs and the archbishops bear the yoke of Christ. The Holy Father in this matter, regarding himself as "the Servant of the servants of God" encounters the people of all cultures with the image of the one who is a "Good Shepherd." As a Pastor, he is ready to search for the lost sheep even at the cost of his life (see Jn 10:10). The Bishop of Rome, the patriarchs and archbishops are "victims, *hostias* to be immolated." The Pope ushers in the global world his readiness to pay the price; which the Apostles have paid, to share in the cross of Christ. St. Paul narrates in a passionate way, "We are afflicted in every way but not crushed; perplexed, but not driven to despair; persecuted, but not destroyed; always carrying in the body the death of Jesus, of that the life of Jesus may also be made visible in our bodies" (2 Cor 4:8-10). The Pope is as one who travels globally to show the grace of serving others- a man called "to serve." Jesus Christ tells his disciples, "...but whoever wishes to be great among you must be your servant, and whoever wishes to be first among you must be your slave; just as the Son of Man came not to be served but to serve, and to give his life a ransom for many" (Mt 20:26-28).

Telling the World the Will of God

With the pallium on his shoulders in every Pontifical Mass, the world gets the glimpse of the man, the Pope is. He is the Pastor who carries God's yoke, in other words he brings to the people of all cultures the will of God. He strives to make the will of God known everywhere, to shed the light of hope in every culture. 'To know what God wants, to know where the path of life is found-this was Israel's joy, this was her great privilege. It is also our joy: God's will does not alienate us, it purifies us-even if this can be painful-and so it leads us to ourselves' (Benedict XVI 2005:192). Telling the whole world the will of God implies that the Pope meets the people with a prophetical stance. This is likely to lead into conflict and his becoming a target to destructive forces.

As representative of Jesus Christ the high Priest, the pallium shouldered Pontiff casts to the world an idea that the world is not left alone. It is carried and supported by the Good Shepherd. The pallium reflects the idea that we are all supported by Jesus Christ. Just as Christ carries us and cares for our welfare, so we are required to carry one another. Hence the pallium reminds us of the serene way on which Jesus leads his Church. The yoke of God entrusted to the

Pope and the bishops, who while true to their own weakness and the weakness of the sheep under their care, makes the burden of the pallium they shoulder to act as a compass to embrace "the innocence of the lamb." While the Pope has supreme and universal power over the universal Church, bishops have ordinary, immediate and proper power in their dioceses. The pallium on their shoulders is a signpost that, 'it is not power, but love that redeems us! This is God's sign: he himself is love. How often we wish that God would show himself stronger, that he would strike decisively, defeating evil and creating a better world' (Benedict XVI 2005:193)

Making a journey to all corners around with a pallium on his shoulder, the Pope is a pastor who comes to serve and not be served. He proposes something to the world leaders that leadership is at its best when it is oriented to serve the citizens. It is best when it is guided by the practice of justice. Government that does not work to serve its own people functions like a political syndicate of mercenaries. This type of politicians, brands himself as an elitist only concerned about serving his belly. The pallium sends a message to world leaders to avoid the cult of power and might. The Pope presents to them the God who became a lamb, not as someone who destroys enemies, who seeks vengeance or gives threats and punishments. 'Isaiah condemned Israel for trusting in military alliances with Egypt and her unquestioning conviction that horses and chariots would protect. And yet Israel's sin is the sin of all those nations enslaved to the rebellious principalities and powers, enslaved to the assumption that might makes right' (Camp 2008:94). The Pope, while extending hands to his fellow heads of states and shouldered with pallium, calls for their attention. World leaders should be careful in the way they wield their powers. 'The powers ultimately wielded their ultimate weapon of death - but Jesus obeyed even unto death. His obedience, his simply light led to his suffering...the cross was the consequence of being love and light, and holiness in the midst of a rebellious world of vengeance, and darkness, and lust' (Camp 2008:95).

Finally the pallium adorned Pope dispels the worldly tendency to crown the Pope as one of the world's "super stars." Every Christian faithful knows that the way to discipleship is costly and sometimes, like Jeremiah leads to a state of desperation (see Jer 15:10). The Pope and bishops now face critics and even rebellion. Pastors of the Church are not celebrities; on the contrary they are the image of crucified Christ. Seeing the Pope with pallium on his shoulder remind everyone of the burdens of his high office. It follows that the Catholic faithful must support the Bishop of Rome and all the bishops by prayers and best wishes in their apostolic ministry. The Holy Father invites everyone of the faithful confronting difficult situation to look at Jesus Christ. The Good Shepherd, Jesus Christ tells us "come to me, all you that are weary and are carrying heavy burdens and I will give you rest. Take my yoke upon you, and learn from me; for I am gentle and humble in heart, and you will find rest for your souls. For my yoke is easy, and my burden is light" (Mt 11:28-30).

5

Universal Pastor in Pope Mobiles

During his trips abroad the Pope encounters huge crowds in stadiums using the so called *Pope mobile*. This is an informal name for the specifically designed motor vehicle used by the Pope during outdoor appearances. With the mobile the Pope can have access to thousands of believers who are gathered in a huge area. Usually the people who gather for the Pontifical Mass scatter over a vast area but are partitioned with open roads on which the Pope can easily move around, assisted by the security personnel to greet the people and bless them.

Sheltering the Pope for Security

The invention of the Pope mobile is in view of strengthening the security of the Holy Father. It was felt indispensable after the assassination attempt on the person of Pope John Paul II by Ali Agca. Some Pope mobiles are open; others have bulletproof glass to enclose the Holy Father. There are also the Pope mobiles in which the Pope can sit, while others are designed to accommodate the Pope while standing.

The use of Pope mobile signalled a new era of mobility, and coincides with the advent of the mobile phones. It is a departure from the use of *Sedia gestatoria*, which was the chair carried on the shoulders by a number of papal butlers. This practice was ended during the time of Pope Paul VI. During his visit to address the General Assembly at the UNO headquarters in New York, Pope Paul VI was driven by a car which was manufactured by the Ford Motor Company which was based on the presidential limousine (see *Wikipedia* 2011). The same was reused in 1970 during his visit to

Bogota (Columbia). In some years later, the *Mercedes-Benz* 600 Pullman-Landaulet was used.

To date the Pope mobiles are updated with bulletproof windows, and bombproof parts. The Pope mobile used by Pope Benedict XVI is modified Mercedes-Benz M-Class sport utility vehicle with a special glass-enclosed "room" that has been built into the back of the vehicle. The Pope enters through a rear door and ascends several steps. After the Pope sits in his chair, it is elevated up into the glass "room" by a hydraulic lift, allowing the Pope to be more easily seen. In addition to the driver, there is room for one passenger (usually a security agent) in the front of the vehicle. The glass-enclosed rear of the vehicle has room for two papal aides who can sit in the area in front of the Pope's elevated chair. 'The vehicle's security features include bulletproof glass windows and roof and reinforced, armoured side panels and undercarriage' (*Wikipedia* 2011).

The use of the Pope mobile that transports the Bishop of Rome during the outdoor audiences seems to be more useful. On 6 June 2007, for example, a German man tried to jump into Pope Benedict XVI's uncovered Pope mobile, as the Holy Father began his general audience. The Pope was not hurt and did not even appear to notice that the 27-year-old man had jumped over the protective barrier in the square and had grabbed onto the white Fiat Pope mobile as it drove by. At least eight security officers who were trailing the vehicle as it moved slowly through the square grabbed the man and wrestled him to the ground. The man was later interrogated by Vatican police (see *Wikipedia* 2011).

The term *Pope mobile*, however, did not come into common usage until when John Paul II took on the leadership of the Church. In 2002, Pope John Paul II requested that the media stop referring to the car as the Pope mobile, saying that the term is "undignified" (see *Wikipedia*). In fact John Paul who epitomized the picture of a "travelling Pope" promoted through his many journeys the conception of "Pope mobile." This concept coincides well with the situation we have today of mobility as already mentioned above. The Church, especially, through the Benedictine Order, has given the impression that the holiness is a value linked with one's stability in the monastery, and family home. The *stabilitas loci* (staying in stable manner at the monastery); was a mantra which enabled monks to observe the ideal community life. These includes: the common prayers, the common table fellowship, community meditation of the Word (*lectio divina*), and the *hora sancta;* or *visitatio* (a moment of adoration/or visitation to the Blessed Sacrament). Finally, in the night all monks and nuns retreats together observing the *silencio magna* (big/complete silence), everyone to his or her monastery cell.

In emphasizing the *stabilitas loci* seminarians, monks, and parishioners were exhorted to observe stability. This practice was taken to be ideal and a guarantee for one's security in married life, religious vocations and priestly vocations as well. With this kind of formal discipline, the idea of mobility seems to be worldly and corrupt. But, this is not true. Every Church community has a mission *ad intra* as well as *ad extra*. A family has not to close upon itself; it must outreach the neighbours and relatives. The monastery is not an island; it has a mission *ad extra* as well. This is truly so because the Christian faithful is someone who is "exiled" from his/her homeland. The Greek word *parokia* which has given root to the English word *Parish* stems from two words *para* which is a proposition meaning "alongside," and *oikos* is a noun that means a "dwelling place." A "parishioner," then, is one who lives alongside or near, not inside but at the edge indeed at the margin. The Epistle to Diognetes describes the itinerant characteristics of the Christians in this way: "they live in their own countries, but only as alien *paroikos*! They participate in everything as foreigners. Every foreign country is their fatherland, and every fatherland is foreign" (*Letter to Diognetes*). Mobility in a positive sense is noble. However, it is important to mention that, despite the demands of mobility, mobility without some stability is a form of character disorder, a lack of discipline. Stability without mobility is ineffective, because it is likely to hinder openness with the outside world, prevent new ideas and invention, and block dialogue with the outside world. In this sense we do not think that the term *Pope mobile* in the context of today is undignified.

In Need of the Pope for Security

At this time of major displacement of people marked by internal and international migrations, many families greatly feel the loss of a home. This loss is made stronger by the disappearance of the father image in the family. 'There is in our time a creeping dread of homelessness' (see Bouma-Prediger:Walsh 2008:6). Male parents, especially in the countries of the South are forced now and again to move away from their families. Although the female parents are also displaced, those moving are largely men. The reason behind this reality is financial problems. In the majority of the World or Developing Countries, males have more financial security than women, and to be able to travel, one needs money to pay for the journey. In the South of the globe as in the West, many mothers, for different reasons: divorce, imprisonment of their husbands, or displacement are obliged to care for their children alone. So in many families the frequent question to mothers asked by their children is "Mammy, where is Papa?"

In global Catholicism one feels that more and more people are in need of the reassurance from the Holy Father. And, this is in view of the crisis which has crippled the Church over the years, the threat of secularism and terrorism, and the persecution of minority Christians in some parts of the world. The poor are marginalized and forgotten by the global powers, and are indeed always in search for the support of the Holy Father. In extreme cases, the desperation and the total confusion may lead them to the question "Where are you Holy Father?"

At this time of mobility with mobile phones connecting people from long distances, the anxiety of displacement is enormous. The first question when one receives the mobile call to the person who is well acquainted with is "where are you?" This is the first question which God asked humanity. It is posed after Adam had just broken off from God. As is always the case when we break off from God, after a while God runs after us. God says, "Adam, where are you?" Adam replies, "I was frightened because I was naked, and so I hid."

Three words: fear, nakedness, and hiding (see Hauerwas: Vanier 2008:61).

Therefore the question "where are you?" reveals our feeling of insecurity. We reckon from this question that the traditional links that ensured the stability of society have fallen apart. 'And that estrangement, that culture-wide sense of displacement, is fundamentally a feature of mobility. The migrant's sense of being rootless, of living between worlds, between a lost past and a non-integrated present, is perhaps the most fitting metaphor of this (post) modern condition' (Bouma-Prediger:Walsh 2008:8). The experience of being uprooted is realized by many people who distance themselves from their traditions. The so called grand narratives, dogmas, doctrines, homes, families, are no longer taken as essential components to model our conduct. We have moved away from a traditional point o reference that at one time gave us reassurance.

The Bible teaches us to understand that we have to keep in relationship with God in order to be at home. God himself is the provider of a dwelling for human family. To find peace, security and happiness, the human person must be in harmony with God, fellow human beings and the natural created order. The Bible uses the concept of a "garden" or a paradise to symbolise the primordial home for human beings. The stories we read from Gen 2-11) are moving and humbling. It is a story that moves quickly from a situation of being at home to a state of homelessness. The cause of homelessness is disobedience, a lack of union with God. We find Adam and Eve overstepping the boundaries which God had laid for their security. At the end, they discovered they had no security apart from God. The two find themselves cast out from God's presence. "But the LORD God called to the man, and said to him 'where are you?'"

After the fall the exilic experience begins. Adam and Eve are now away from the Paradise. They have vacated their natural home. The experience of homelessness exposes one to the feeling of vulnerability. 'If home is a resting place, a place of security and comfort, exile is the deepest and most devastating experience of homelessness' (Bouma-Prediger: Walsh 2008: 20). The estrangement of Adam and Eve is both at physical and spiritual. Adam and Eve's relationship with God has diminished because of their sin, and as a result they hide. They do not feel safe or secure any longer (see Goliama 2011:196). They have discovered their brokenness; no longer do they have the same integrity they harboured before. Clothing their naked bodies designed from the beginning with natural beauty symbolizes running away from the sight of God. It begins the era of human displacement in history. It inaugurates instability for human families. Adam's answer reveals a spiritual rupture as it clearly portrays the awareness of both of them that they have divorced themselves from the Creator who desires companionship with them. (see Goliama 2011:196).

After the fall human beings experience a radical disruption which affected the relational levels: relationship between God and humanity, humanity and creation, and man and woman. As a result of this fraction of harmony is a restless search for *shalom*. After the fall comes the experience that the peace that was enjoyed at Paradise is no longer a normative state of creation, but it is a projection in the future.

Human beings who are made in God's image are no longer secure. In his abundant love, however, God takes part in the history of displacement, to rescue the fallen human being. He sends then his own Son born of the woman, the new Adam to redeem fallen humankind. He is born as the *Letter to the Hebrews* states, to fulfil the will of God, namely to save people from the yoke of sin. "Then I said, see God, I have come to do your will, O God" (Heb 10:7). The new Adam, is introduced at his baptism in the Jordan river as someone who is beloved and one who pleases his Father; "This is my Son, the Beloved, with who I am well pleased" (Mt 3:17). According to St. John, the Son is someone who is sent to fulfil the will of his Father (see Jn 5:37). This will is fulfilled by enduring the sufferings on the cross. It is at this hour of suffering and death that is at the same time the hour of his glorification: "And what should I say - Father, save me from this hour? No, it is for this reason that I have come to this hour. Father, glorify your name." Then a voice came from heaven, "I have glorified it, and I will glorify it again" (Jn 12:27-29). For being obedient to the Father until death on the cross, Jesus can faithfully answer the question of God, "Where Are You?" He can on behalf of humanity answer, "Here I am, send me Lord" (see 1 Sam 3:16). As new Adam Jesus Christ establishes a new humanity. He is the principle of all new creation and new birth. Jesus offers something fundamentally and distinctively new from what has gone wrong before him, his life is decisive for the future destiny of humanity.

There is a connection between the old Adam and New Adam. The old Adam following his tragic fall was driven from the garden, the Paradise, which according to early Christian legend, was in Jerusalem. The legend holds that the old Adam was buried on the very spot where Jesus of Nazareth (the new Adam) was crucified. This explains why in some paintings and stained-glass windows across many churches in the world, we see Adam's skull at the foot of the cross. This link between the two Adams also connects the incarnation and resurrection events. From the Christ's event it has become possible now for the human body to be capable of the glory, the attainment of a glorious beauty which originates from God. In his obedience to God, Jesus Christ, has also made possible the human act to be liberated from sin, to reflect the goodness which is God Himself.

As the Vicar of Christ on earth, the Pope preaches to the human family about the new life through Christ. The visits of the Pope to meet people of all cultures in this era of displacement, is pastorally and spiritually very important for all. As the Holy Father sets out on his journey away from Rome, he knows very well the dangers all travellers face on the way. From tradition, being on the road and travelling were considered harmful and dangerous by many people. Blaise Pascal, the French philosopher wrote, "All men's miseries derive from not being able to sit in a quiet room alone" (*Pensées* II, 139). On the occasion of the Third International Conference on Pastoral Care for Roadways in Bogotá, in October 2008, the retired

Secretary of the Pontifical Council for the Pastoral Care of Migrants and Itinerant People Msgr. Agostino Marchetto, explained: "we must be conscious that there is a war on the roadways of the entire world, where every day, hundreds of people die for many different reasons. Immediate intervention is needed to reduce the number of victims" (see Miehle 2010:41). But the Pope is also aware that those in distant places are also members of the Church (see *Lumen Gentium*, no. 13), the faithful who needs his care and encouragement.

In the world of extreme human degradation through the trafficking of human persons, modern slavery is alive in the form of the pornography trade, child prostitution, and sex tourism. Many poor people feel empty. The victim finds themselves deprived of their dignity. They are being treated like garbage. Those who have exploited the poor discover inside their hearts that something has not gone well. Their consciences should tell them what they have done to the poor is unjust. Spiritually, both the victims of injustices and those who have committed injustices, recognize that something is wrong somewhere. They feel everyone in their own way has a sense of not belonging. The victims and their exploiters recognize the "strangeness" in their behaviours as human beings. There is feeling of guilty conscience for some, and hopelessness for the other. Given the situation such as we have today, many people confront the same predicament which the Psalmist had in the past which led him to ask, while rising his eyes high on the mountain as if in desperation: "from where shall my help come?" (see Ps. 121:1)

The papal visits as Vicar of Christ help many people of good will to find the answer to the fundamental questions. The presence of the Holy Father among the people beaten by injustices may help them understand the fact that, Jesus Christ himself has on behalf of all humanity answered God, "here I am to fulfil your will." In Christ the human family has been gathered together as one family. This has special meaning today in a world which preaches divisions between people. Some politicians put emphasis on politics that stresses national identity. Taking France for example, '*The New York Times* described the spring 2007 presidential campaign as seized by a subject long monopolized by the extreme right: how best to be French. Conservative Nicolas Sarkozy proposed a "ministry of immigration and national identity," and Socialist Ségolène Royal advocated memorizing "La Marseillaise" and displaying the French flag on Bastille Day' (Hanson 2011:219). The Pope does not work on such polarizing politics, but as pastor he exhorts all humanity to mutually care. The Bishop of Rome on visiting different countries takes seriously the concerns and pastoral needs of the people there.

Judging secular leaders from some of their policies, one can conclude that they seem to take lightly the social diversity of their own people. They sacrifice the care of ecology for economic gains. 'Our present leaders - people of wealth and power-do not know what it means to take place seriously: to think it worthy, for its own sake, of love and careful work. They cannot take any place seriously because they must be ready at any moment, by the terms of power and wealth in the modern world, to destroy any place' (Bouma-Prediger: Walsh 2008:6). Their citizens discover the superficiality in some of their political discourses. It is no wonder that papal rallies are full of people who come many hours to designated grounds and some even from distant places. Those who join papal masses do so willingly. Many of them feel immense joy standing in long queue waving the Pope. The papal assembly is not a political party ideological gathering. Those who take part do not expect the guest of Rome to give them promises of better performance and to reduce church tax when he arrives back in Rome, for example. The Pope, bishops and priests preach Jesus Christ, the crucified. And therefore, the jubilation such as, *viva il Papa*, "*Be-ne-de-tto we love you*," which the crowd compliments the Pope is a true sentiment springing from the heart. There is an in-depth hilarity in encountering the visitor from Rome. The Christian faithful discovers in the Pope; a Father who protects the weak and the strong, safeguards the unborn, and opposes to bloodshed all the time.

6

Head of State not like others

One of the driving points for the concern of the security of the Pope is in his holding of the position as the head of state. As is the case in all countries, the security of the head of state consumes a lion share of the statehouse budget. This is however not the case with the Vatican State.

The Vatican State is the smallest one in the world. It was started in 1929 after World War I (1914-1918). Pope Pius XI signed the Lateran Treaty with Italy, creating a new independent state governed by the Holy See. The Pope is the head of this state. The creation of this state meant that the Bishop of Rome is not only a pastor of the Catholic Church, but he is internationally recognized, as head of the Holy See. It is for that, the security of the Pope is not only the concern of the administration of the Vatican, but also of the nation - states.

The Pope and His Cabinet

At the very outset of the new government, the world waits to listen to the first speech of the newly elected President. The first speech provides a vision of what the government will be. In the political domain all over the world governments are put in place by the people. The government officials and politicians work hard to satisfy the needs and demands of the voters. These are the ones who have put them in power. Politicians are inclined to serve the interest of the political parties they represent. Political parties vie to win many parliamentary seats in order to be eligible to choose the government. The scramble for power means that the political playground will not always be fair. Manipulations, lies and corruption tarnish politicians as they strive for seats in the government.

The Pope as head of state is not elected to serve "party interest" and unlike other heads of states, his first speech at the balcony of St. Peter is a humbling one. One thinks of Pope John XXIII considering himself completely unsuitable for the post of the Pontiff telling the cardinals, bishops, priests and the people of God all the world over, "at this time of history the Holy Spirit has decided to lead the Church himself," or Benedict XVI telling the crowd at St. Peters square, "after the great Pope John Paul II, God has now chosen, a simple and humble labourer in the vineyards of the Lord."

Those elected to become the successor of Peter tremble because of the greatness of the office and the heavy burden placed on their shoulders. They stand before God who is great Judge, remembering what Michelangelo the painter had portrayed on the ceiling overhead the Sistine chapel. It is the drawings of the Last Judgment. The conclave that elects the Pope is called by the cardinal electors as "the room of tears" (see Benedict 2010:20). The newly elected Pope begins a ministry not to win people for himself but for Christ. The elected Pope does not emerge as a celebrity, as secular leaders do. Politicians celebrate their respective party's victory in some cases behaving like rock stars. They entertain verbal eloquence, body gestures with arousing styles, and appeals to the public for acknowledgement. What is at play is fame and promises of better performances guided by their own power of vision in accordance to their respective party's manifesto. The first appearance of the Pope at the balcony of St. Peters' cathedral, offers a calm presentation of an "ecce homo" style. After serving the Church in different capacities for many years, the cardinal elected Pope would better choose to go to retirement, but now all of the sudden is given a highest responsibility in the Church. It humbles. The newly elected Bishop of Rome appears at the balcony recalling what St. Paul writes: "When I came to you, brothers and sisters I did not come proclaiming the mystery of God in lofty words or wisdom...I came to you in weakness and in fear and in much trembling..." (I Cor 2:1-4).

For secular head of states and politicians what comes in the first place is what one must do next in order to satisfy the voters.

Immediately after being assured of victorious election, conferences with journalists will be called, and speeches are given to extol voters promising to deliver more than previous governments. Meanwhile dinners to congratulate new ministers and members of parliament are organized.

The priority of the Pope is to fulfil what God wants for humanity. The newly elected Bishop of Rome takes time to "retreat" for prayers and fasting before the installation ceremony at the Chair of Peter. Pope Benedict XVI for example, made clear in his first homily during his installation: 'My real programme of governance is not to do my own will, not to pursue my own ideas, but to listen, together with the whole Church, to the world and to the will of the Lord, to be guided by Him, so that He Himself will lead the Church at this hour of our history' (Benedict VI 2005:191).

Considering that, it is important, therefore, to know something about those who elect the Holy Father. What kind of vocation do these electors of the Pope have that determine the criterion guiding them to elect the Bishop of Rome? To know any government well and how it works and what it seeks to achieve one has to look at the cabinet of ministers which the president puts in place to head various ministries. One has to examine the competence of the Prime Minister, and those occupying key ministries such as the Foreign Affairs, Defence, and Finance. A careful choice of these persons may give the picture of how the government is going to deliver to the nation. When the president is surrounded by a team of competent and dedicated ministers, h/she is going to achieve much during his term of office.

The Advent of the Sacred College of Cardinals

As head of the Vatican, the Pope leads the Holy See through the assistance of the Secretary of the State who is a Cardinal. The day to day activities of the State are taken care by different ministries known as Congregations, in ecclesiastical terms. These Congregations are headed by Cardinals called the Prefects of the Congregations. They are identified as: the Congregation of the Doctrine of the Faith, the Congregation of Oriental Churches, the Congregation of Divine Worship and the Discipline of Sacraments, the Congregation of the Causes of Saints, the Congregation of the Evangelization of People, the Congregation of the Clergy, the Congregation of the Institutes of Consecrated life and Societies of Apostolic Life, Congregation of Catholic Education, and the Congregation of Bishops.

It is compelling to trace the history of the College of Cardinals, and learn what kind of governance the Vatican is managing through them. In the primitive Church, the bishops were elected by the priests and lay people. The procedure to elect the Bishop of Rome, however, was not the responsibility of all priests and lay people, but it fell on the Parish priests of major parishes and the deacons who assisted the Pope. These Parish priests of the major parishes around Rome were given the name "Cardinals, because they had a fixed role and played a key role in the life of Church community. They were distinguished as Cardinal Priests and Cardinal Deacons. Later on the Bishops who governed the dioceses surrounding the city of Rome joined the College of Cardinals with the title of Cardinal Bishops.

Given the privileges which the Church enjoyed from the Empire, the cardinals compared themselves to the old Roman Senate and were referred to as the "Princes of the Church." The powers of the Pope extended beyond the ecclesiastical domain. The practice of consulting the College of Cardinals became common. The Pope and cardinals functioned in close collaboration, similar to the royal courts of Europe during the middle Ages. The cardinals, however, were entitled to elect the Pope; and for that they took part in a kind of democratic election of their leader, which many types of nobility in Europe did not have. The secular nobilities appeared solemnly in royal garments during public functions, but had no power to elect or depose the monarchical king.

In 1150 during the pontificate of Pope Eugene III, the cardinals formed the "Sacred College," which was under the presidency of its Dean; with Carmelengo Cardinal as chief economist and procurator of the affairs of the papal household. In 1179 during the Lateran

Council III, it was decided that the election of the Pope should be done by the majority two third of the electors, to avoid contestation about the legitimacy of the Pope's election which in extreme cases had caused schism in the Church.

Church Dignitaries in Red Purple

Cardinals wear a red cassock, a red *Biretta*, including a red *cingulum*. The red colour is very significant to understand the nature of the cabinet, which the Pope has. The garment of the Pope throughout the middle ages was red, until the time of Pope Pius V (1566-1572). At the time of his election he appeared with red garments like the Cardinals who elected him. During his election to the pontificate, Pope Pius V who was a Dominican, decided to put on the white cassock to honour the Dominican Order. His intention was to appreciate the mendicant Order that gave him the spirituality to even be trusted to the greatest office in the Church. From then on the popes who followed him decided to distinguish themselves with white robes. In special function however, the Pope puts on a Red *Mozetta*. During holidays he puts on a big red hat, and wears red shoes.

The red colour is at the same time a symbol of blood and fire. It is a sign of life, power, force and sacrifice. In the ancient Rome the colour purple was the colour of generals, of patriots, and it was reserved to the emperor and those close to him. The emperor Constantine was completely vested in red. It was Pope Innocent IV who in 1244 permitted his cardinals to carry a red hat. From then onwards the red colour has been associated with the dignity of cardinals. By wearing red cassocks and Biretta, the Pope and cardinals bear a sign that they are ready to shed their blood to defend the Catholic faith. The newly appointed cardinals are given a ring by the Pope. The ring has the portrait of Mary the Mother of the Church and of the apostles Peter and Paul, two indispensable pillars in the Church. What is portrayed in the cardinal ring is significant, given that; 'the Petrine ministry of office,...the Pauline ministry of theologizing and evangelization- the kingly, priestly, and prophetic offices, if you will- are all finally reducible to the Marian form' (Barron 2011:98).

The city of Rome is a custodian of the graves of St. Peter and St. Paul. It has a number of catacombs where Christian martyrs who died for their faith are buried. The red colour reminds the cardinals of their way to martyrdom. Therefore, the cabinet of the Pope is made up of distinguished prelates without security; for all of them are witnesses for the truth. In other words, by living the Christian wisdom, through their bold witness of the faith, and their unwavering obedience to the Pope, cardinals set an example for all the Christians. They are globally a "persecuted minority."

Audiences from the Window

The Pope has weekly audiences with pilgrims who visit the Vatican. Some of these audiences are of official nature. They are organized on Wednesdays in the St. Paul VI's audience hall, which can accommodate a relatively big number of people. For small groups, especially for Church and State dignitaries the audiences are given in the private library. Otherwise, the Pope makes an audience to the huge crowd in public at St. Peter's square, and on Sundays also from the window of his own apartment.

Windows communicate to us much of what we can conclude about a particular building. In some church buildings, windows inform a curious visitor about a deep treasure of the Gospels. Looking at the windows in different churches, one is fascinated by the spirituality ushered through paintings. Symbols and image portraits on church windows helps the faithful understand much. Paintings make a thrilling impression about the painters themselves. From such windows one discovers a human person, the painter is gifted at praying, a *homo orans* and with artistic talent of painting a *homo faber*. The painter appears to be in dialogue with the creation and is fascinated by the beauty of creation; thus being capable of loving it, hence a *homo amans*. Church windows give the idea that, the whole building is a place for prayer. Windows furnish spiritual meditations for church visitors.

A story loved by preachers many be illuminating at this juncture. A group of tourists were visiting a huge cathedral. A little girl in the group stopped, in contemplative silence, to look at the beautiful huge stained glass window. The afternoon sun was shining brightly, bathing the group in a splendid symphony of gorgeous colours. After some time, as the group was about to leave, the little girl asked the guide, "who are those persons in those beautiful windows?" The guide told her that they were the saints. That evening, as the little girl prepared for bed, she told her mom that she knew who the saints were. "Well, who are they?" her mother wanted to know. "Saints are persons who let light shine through them!" was her innocent reply

Windows are informative. When they are shut we are prevented to see through, we are possibly not allowed inside. In opening the window of his study room, one discovers the good will of the Bishop of Rome. Usually, secular head of states addresses the citizens in much safer places where they are surrounded by security personnel. It poses a security risk to address the people from a window. From the window the Pope is visible to almost everyone present at St. Peter's Square. One can understand why Pope Paul VI wanted to discontinue the custom of the papal audience from his private room. Asked about this issue Pope Benedict XVI offers a careful and theological backing for such practice:

> Yes, I understand the feelings of Paul VI very well. Here is the question: Is it really right for someone to present himself again and again to crowd in that way and allow oneself to be regarded as a star? On the other hand, people have an intense longing to see the Pope. It is not so much a question then of contact with the person as it is of being physically in touch with this office, with the representative of the Holy One, with the mystery that there is a successor to Peter and someone who must stand for Christ. In this sense, then, one has to accept it and not refer the jubilation to oneself as a personal compliment (Benedict 2010:77).

The papal audiences from the window are always done on Sundays after the noon high mass. The pilgrims gather at St. Peter's and anxiously wait for the window to open. When the Pope is in the Vatican, pilgrims recognize the possibility to have an audience with him especially when they find a red flag that bears the emblem of the reigning Pope lowered underneath the window of the papal apartment. This is to underline his magisterial authority in the allocations delivered to the audience.

During such audiences the Pope speaks with pilgrims from different countries. At major solemnities like Easter and Christmas, the Pope greets the people of different nations in major world languages from all the five continents. The window depicts the Pope's global outreach commitment. The Bishop of Rome, as pastor of the universal Church, is not biased. Communicating with people in different languages shows that he is a head of states unlike others. He treats all the people with the politeness of Pentecost, in the event where everyone heard the apostles speaking in one's own tongue.

One of the distinguished marks for the head of nation states is their ability to communicate in their own languages. The official language of the President of the United States of America is English. Regardless whether he is conversant in Kiswahili for example, when he visits Kenya, he is going to address the people in English. The German Chancellor will use the German language, and also the Russian President, who will use the Russian language and so forth. Even if Latin is the official language of the Roman Catholic Church, it the Pope is not bound to speak in the Latin or Italian languages when travelling outside Italy. He communicates with the people in their own language. Thus, from the window of the papal apartment symbolically the Church opens itself to the world.

The catholicity nature of the Church is made clear particularly by Radio Vatican owned by the Holy See. It was founded in 1931 and it broadcasts now in more than 50 languages. There is no media owned by a nation state with such openness. People in communist countries such as North Korea and China can hear Radio Vatican airing in their own languages, and those in Islamic countries such as Afghanistan and Bahrain can also be accessed in the Arabic language. This is exactly what the Greek word *Katholon* which is the etymological origin of the English word *Catholic* seems to convey.

Audiences from the window are done from the Pope's private study room. As teacher and pastor, the Pope is committed to constant studying. In principle he is a man of prayer, contemplation and studies. A life of constant studies is indispensable for the Pope, bishops and priests in their pursuit of truth. As they are charged with the teaching office of the mother Church, studying becomes like a "quasi sacrament" in the lives of the pastors. In opening the window of his study room and delivering speeches of encouragement to the world, the Pope makes his study room the place of spiritual and academic charity. The Pope extends the generosity of Christian wisdom through preaching, writing, and giving allocutions.

The opening of the window of his study room shows to the world what kind of head of state, the Bishop of Rome is. The Pope's study room generates a Christian fraternal imagination. After the fall of Adam and Eve the human experience of hospitality is twisted between two social categories; each informed by evasion of the hospitality of God. In the first category God's hospitality is experienced as absent in a final, mocking way. As life situation is marked by deep sin and division there is a deep resentment which abandons many in a desert of disorientation and despair. All over the world many people feel like flotsam, washed up on a beach. They feel like aliens in their own homes. The danger in this social category is the fact that hospitality is displayed as "restoration campaign" aimed at rehabilitating a "lost public image." Dinners and suppers organized may tend to be a kind of self reparation, with the intention to reinstate a good image. The second social category is gripped with a sense of despair. The hospitality of God is denied and dismissed. Human beings usurp a "complete freedom" away from the Creator. Such atmosphere makes human beings live between despair and pride. In most cases hospitality forges patronage and control over others.

The Pope and the faithful gathered at his palace offer a different narrative to appreciate the hospitality of God. This caring and life giving hospitality is revealed in the person of Jesus Christ. It is provides life to the full (see Jn 10:10). The liberating hospitality is at once public (that is made open to all) and personal. It moves beyond racial, ethnic, status and faith orientation. One observes that the papal apartment is filled with people from all over the world. The pilgrims yearn for an inner experience of Christ. The opening of the papal window and the presence of Pope in person, gathers the people from different parts of the world. It feels like a spiritual family. The pilgrims assemble before the Pope at noon time for prayers. It is a time when many families prepare at table for meals. This is an appropriate moment to bring forth the appreciation of God's hospitality. What the Pope shows during the audience is the obligation of the family of God to sanctify time. At St. Peter's square, pilgrims know that their journey to Rome has a very significant meaning in their life time. The setting off on a journey in its different ways- travelling (on foot, bus, train, etc) is connected with time- and for that is deeply associated with the mystery of the incarnation.

The midday offers a special opportunity to recall with gratitude the Word of God taking human flesh in world history and becoming one of us. The *Angelus* prayer gives the incarnation a specific accent. Only after sanctifying the time by praying together then the Christian family can get together at table having already fulfilled this noble duty. As Eucharistic community the Catholic faithful know that they are eaters of the graceful food. The spiritual food is shared and so is the physical food at family table. The food we share liberates us from the illusion of abundant mirage, which drives us to control others and to the passion to accumulate more. We learn through prayer how to receive food as gift and not as a guaranteed stuff available at dictation.

From the explanations given at the paragraph above one may reckon as to why in many Catholic churches, the bells ring at midday to summon families to pray the *Angelus*. Drawing a lesson from the lives of monks and nuns, we learn that the taking of breakfast follows the *Laudes* (morning prayers) and the Mass; with the Benedictines for example, lunches are taken immediately after the (*Nona*) afternoon prayers, and supper is shared after the *Vespers* (the evening prayers). From the tradition of the Church over many centuries the Christians have always taken short pause for prayer at the noon hour. From the apostolic times, the noon prayer was addressed as the prayer of the "sixth hour," as people counted time from sunrise. In the book of the Act of Apostles we are informed that St. Peter was praying the noontime prayers when he received a revelation from the Lord (see Acts 10:9).

The opening of the window has a symbolical meaning of the Church which is prepared to meet the secular world. An opened window allows a new fresh air to fill the house. This may apply to mean that the Church welcomes fresh ideas and stands ready to learn from the world. She is ready to listen and engage with the world. The opening of the window in this line assists the Church to read the signs of the time. It is symbolic, for it reflects the vigilance which the Church as a pilgrim community is called to live. Even at moments of insecurity such as we have today, the Church has to open herself to initiate fraternal ties among the people.

The Vatican Flag: An Emblem of Peace

In every country the national flag is an important emblem of every nation state. The colour of the flag represents something about the values which the particular nation seems to uphold. It speaks also about the security and peace of the nation. To know about the nature of a particular nation state it is important to learn about the national flag.

The Vatican State has its own flag, which is known all over the world. It has a long history. The flag is one of only two square country flags in the world, the other being the flag of Switzerland, the country known for its peace and neutrality in world politics. The flag consists of vertical bands, one of gold (hoist side) and one of white.

It was adopted in 1929, in the Italian state constitution. The flag was first flown by the Papal States merchant ships from 1825-1870.

The flag has two colours. 'Yellow and white have been the papal colours since 1808 when they were first used in a cockade, i.e. a circular cloth badge' (Becker 2008:1). Yellow and white colours have a positive meaning in many cultures. In many countries including Tanzania, the yellow colour stands for peace. The Tanzanian national flag has a yellow colour as one of the four colours, which marks the peaceful transition towards its independence in 1961. The white colour signifies peace and innocence. The white colour draws symbolism throughout the Bible equating white clothes with purity and forgiveness. It depicts the status of Christians who following the way of their master of martyrdom have been washed like snow. In this sense the white colour seeks to usher the biblical description of Jesus' non violence and surrender to God's will. In different parts of the world, when the Vatican flag is flown, the people conceive of the idea of a peaceful State.

Within the white colour there are two keys of St. Peter, crossed diagonally. These keys have been a papal emblem since the middle ages (see Becker 2008:1). They refer to the words Jesus spoke to Simon Peter after he acknowledged him to be the Messiah, "...I will give you the keys of the kingdom of heaven, and whatever you bind on earth will be bound in heaven, and whatever you loose on earth will be loosed in heaven" (Mt 16:19). The popes are regarded as successors of St. Peter, and the gold and silver keys have been significant elements in the symbolism of the papal state since the 13th century. The gold represents spiritual power, while the silver key represents worldly power. A red cord, symbolizes the martyrdom nature of this power, which connects the two keys. On top of it is the sign of the cross. One is also able to find in this red cord, the anchor image in Christianity symbolize the faith. The fact that this is connected with two keys expresses clearly the role of the successor of Peter to preserve the doctrine of the Church, even to the extent of shedding blood. The red cord is made up like the Wager (Balance) which symbolizes the dispensation of justice. The Pope has also the duty to dispense justice, and for that he represents God the Final Judge who is just and merciful.

These keys are crowned with a tiara. The triple tiara has been a papal symbol since the middle ages, with various symbolic interpretations. The dominant theory holds that the three crowns in the tiara represent the Pope's supremacy over other earthly head of states. For many years the popes have used the tiara-keys emblem. However, the last Pope to wear an actual tiara was Paul VI. He sold the tiara and disposed the money to help the poor in the world.

A Pastor Not Commander in Chief

The Pope is foremost a pastor. He is not like the other heads of states. We mentioned already at the beginning that the Pope has no Defence Forces, like a national army as in nation states. This means that the Pope does not bear the title of Commander in Chief.

A State without Military Force

Vatican is a State without the military force. This is especially reflected in the composition of senior officers of the Roman curia. The Holy See does not have the "Congregation for the Security of the Holy See," for example. This means that the Pope does not have to appoint Generals, Chief of Defence Forces, Inspector General of the Police Forces, and the Commissioner of Prisons. The Vatican has no Prisons Department Service. It has no Field Force Unit either.

The Holy Father does not have a team of Security Advisors whom he can convene at any time to discuss about the security of the Vatican State. He lacks the pride of other heads of states who boast of their large armies and sophisticated weaponry. Every nation state ensures the presence of Special Forces which are called to rescue the president and to guarantee the security of the nation in case of need. One thinks here of the special presidential guards, special marines, army commandos, etc. All these forces are highly trained and endure extreme physical and psychological examinations to be well suited for most delicate missions. One also thinks of the Field Force unit called when there is a public unrest to bring order. All these forces are important in situations of insecurity.

Historically, however, there was a time when the Pope owned a small military unit. From 1850 the Vatican had a military unit which was called the *Palatine Guard*. It was founded by Pope Pius IX. These corps was established as an infantry unit, to help in the defence of Rome. After the first Vatican Council (1869-1870), following the unification of Italy, the Palatine Guard was confined to the Vatican City where they performed ceremonial functions as guard of honour. This body of soldiers was seen especially when the Pope was in St. Peter's square or when important visitors were received by the Pope. Those who were recruited in the corps were lay volunteers who were not paid for their service. It was a simple military group without sophisticated weapons. This army lacked modern weapons and the guardsmen received little training. The army was the only one in the service of the Vatican to have a full military band. The Palatine Guard was abolished in 1970. The Pope has a simple body of a police force that guard the Holy See. The policemen assure the safety of the temporal goods of the Vatican State. During the feast of the Archangels Michael, Gabriel and Raphael, that is celebrated on the 29th September of every year the Vatican police make a parade on the square to pronounce their commitment to protect the august person of the Holy Father. Besides the small group of police the Vatican State has a ceremonial security network known as "the Swiss Guards."

The Swiss Guards at the Vatican

The Swiss Guard is a contingent of about 110 men, under one commander, one chaplain, three officers, 25 lesser officers and 80 guards. These men are all Swiss citizens and Catholics of good reputation. For acceptance into the Guard, the men must be unmarried, between 19 and 30 years of age and at least 5 feet, 8 inches tall (174 cm). There is a minimum commitment of two years of service, and during these initial years, the guards must remain celibate. Those who decide to extend their mandate may be allowed to marry depending on the availability of accommodation.

The main function of the Swiss Guards is the protection of the person of the Holy Father. The members of the Guard are responsible for the custody of the entrance to the apostolic palaces, the papal apartments and the Pope's summer residence of Castelgandolfo. They protect the Pope during solemn pontifical ceremonies, during which they also guard the chapels. In years past, six members of the Guard would flank the Pope as he was carried on the *Sedia gestatoria*. Today, when the Roman Pontiff travels abroad, several plain-clothed members of the Swiss Guard accompany him, along with members of the Vatican police. The ceremonial weapon of the Guardsmen is the seven-foot-long medieval boarding pike or halberd. However, when they are with the Pope during his foreign visits, they often have a fire weapon, a personal revolver.

From history, the popes had used the Swiss soldiers for the protection of the Holy See since the late 14th century. It was, however, not until the Pontificate of Julius II (1503-13), that the papal Swiss Guard was officially formed. Through Cardinal Matthäus Schiner, Julius II negotiated a treaty with the cantons of Zürich and Lucenne, and on June 21, 1505, he requested that 200 soldiers be sent to Rome with Peter von Hertenstein as Captain and Caspar von Silenen as Commander. From the time of the Renaissance the uniform of the Swiss Guard consists of dark blue, red and yellow colours with a white collar. Traditionally, Michelangelo the famous Italian painter is credited with the design, but some dispute this claim. Tourists frequently wish to have their photographs taken with members of the Guard. The Swiss Guards are allowed to take photographs with the tourists who ask them to do so, when security risks are minimal.

On May 6 of each year; there is a solemn ceremony which includes the swearing in of the new members of the Swiss Guard. The oath is taken in one of the Swiss languages-German, French, Italian and Ladino-the soldiers raise three fingers of their right hand in honour of the Trinity and place their left hand on the flag of the Swiss Guard Corps. The flag is made up of a large white Swiss cross and three shields representing the coat of arms of the present Pope, Pope Julius II, the founder of the Swiss Guard, and the current commander of the Guards. A long historical tradition has held that the Commander of the Guard is a member of the Swiss nobility, but in recent years this tradition has not been followed. The oath taken on 6 May pledges fidelity to the Pope his successors, and to the College of Cardinals when See of Peter is vacant. The members of the Guard likewise pledge to dedicate themselves to the service and defence of the Popes even, if necessary, by the sacrifice of their lives.

Therefore, the Swiss Guards is not an attacking force. It is not crafted like other military and police forces, to face and crush the enemies. It is not a fully established army like in other states; which usually composed of sections ranging from: companies, platoons, barracks, brigade commands, and the national force. Its members are not ranked from the lower grade composed of recruits and privates/service men and women. And from this low ranks, the next grade is made up of junior officers made up of corporals, sergeants, lieutenants and captains. At the top of the command are senior officer's team which includes: the majors, brigadiers, major generals, generals and field marshals.

The Swiss Guard lacks the litany of ranks enumerated above which elaborate and characterizes an attacking force. To efficiently wage an attack against the enemy of the state, the military must be divided into an infantry division that is to advance and face the enemy at the ground combats. The Air Force takes charge and surveillance of the airspace. The Navy force on its part is responsible to secure the waters of a particular nation. Such an army must have its own military police to enforce discipline in the barracks or the special force made up of highly intelligent and well trained elites to be deployed in difficult missions. The Vatican security corpus is a very small force with no other mission than protecting the life of the Holy See and guarding the Vatican compounds. With its pacifist policy the Vatican State never prejudges anyone as an enemy and excludes no one who is made in the image of God. Thus Robert Mugabe though, prohibited by the European Union to visit Europe, yet could take part at the funeral of Pope John Paul II in 2005. To the attackers of Church personnel and those against the teachings of the Church, the Pope and bishops do not pronounce threats against them like secular leaders, who at critical moments call for international manhunt of their pronounced enemies: "Wanted dead or alive." What comes from the Church is an immediate appeal for reconciliation and dialogue. No recourse to economic sanctions, no ultimatum with military punishments. The Vatican trusts that goodness is to reign at last. The Vatican State, therefore, has no worries to place security items like radars to protect its air space for example. St. Peter's Square is not a place for military power; rather it is a space to cement fraternity in Christ.

Security Cordon: or a Fear Syndrome?

The Pope puts unwavering trust in divine assistance in protecting him. For that the security personnel attached for his personal safety is very limited. Pope Benedict XVI highlights the experience on his trips abroad, 'the trips are very demanding for me...but that I am simply there for the Lord-and that I don't need to worry' (Benedict XVI 2010:108). This makes quite a big difference with the security measure which is afforded to secular leaders.

When paying visits to other countries the guest head of states, after a ceremonial welcome at the airport, presidential motorcades begins with traffic police on white motorcycles. These are assisted by a section of uniformed security members of the army, and security personnel in plain clothes. Some line along the high way to prevent the people from crossing over. The security system, as a whole, portrays state's supremacy. It displays at the same time the sovereign power of the state. The security personnel surrounding the heads of states send a clear message to would be "security breakers" that they will be crushed in kind. The provision of tight security which is accorded to the head of states imagines an enemy and speaks louder of the disposition for confrontation.

Everywhere in the world presidential convoys portray in convenient way inherent insecurity gripping nation states and its heads. In Uganda for example, Joshua Mmali, BBC correspondent in Kampala reports that President Yoweri Museveni travels in a convoy of uncountable vehicles, with an ambulance and a huge mobile toilet – no matter where he's going...Here you see military guys on pick-up trucks with weapons threateningly pointing at other road users in order to intimidate them (see *BBC Focus on Africa* April-June 2012:24).

It may be interesting to pick another example from the visit the President of the United States made in Great Britain. During the May 2011, when President Barack Obama visited England, the security cordon was incredible. The surveillance in the air, on the road, and in the food and health assurance was done to the maximum. This visit coincided with his ordering of the raid that killed Osama Bin Laden, and the subsequent threat by the *Al Qaida* network to retaliate, made the provision of his security one of the tightest ever to be mounted in the United Kingdom. Sniffer dogs were deployed to hunt for explosives, while officials checked for evidence of chemical or biological threats. The Air Forces control was highly sophisticated to ensure the President arrived safely. As President and his wife Michelle arrived at the Stansted Airport on Air Force One, a modified Boeing 747 the VH-3D helicopters were flown by US Marine corps pilots and were flown in groups of identical helicopters, with as many as four decoys (see *BBC News* 2011). These choppers are capable of firing flares to divert heat-seeking missiles, have twin engines and are equipped to deal with surface-to-air and air-to-air attacks. The United Kingdom forces took the responsibility to clear its air space (see *BBC News* 2011).

On the roads which the President was scheduled to pass British police cars and motorbikes led the way, alongside with US agents, to secure the route, followed by the secret service vehicles, support cars and emergence medical vehicles. To camouflage the Presidential limousine were three to four- vehicle groups, and at its centre is the armoured limousine. Nicknamed "The Beast", this modified Cadillac has been described as the safest vehicle on the planet, assembled at a cost of $ 3000,000 (£ 186,000). It has 20cm (eight inch) armour-plated doors and tyres that still work after being shot through (see *BBC News* 2011). In the Presidential convoy followed the counter-assault car, which had the job of attacking any hostile threat. As regards food and health the American President was accompanied with a team of chefs who prepared his food-apart from that served at the official functions- both for convenient and security. The health of the President had to be assured by a team of qualified medical team, equipped with a supply of his blood type AB (see BBC News 2011).

This way of protecting the American President differs greatly from the security plans for the Pope who is a Pastor. He has to bless the people; he has to listen to the sick people and pose before mothers who bring their babes to him. Like Jesus Christ, the Pope must tell the parents to let the children come to him. He cannot just bless such babes from his enclosed bullet proof Pope mobile. Sometimes he opens the window and kisses the babes, shake hands with their mothers. In doing so the Pope must be prepared to put his life in danger.

It is a paradox the President of the most powerful nation should be treated with uppermost care in view of the profound sense of insecurity. For the American head of state, who is chosen by voters and who preaches democracy and freedom all over the world, ideally he should win the support of the people and hardly have enemies. Yet the opposite is true. 'The United States is the strongest nation on the face of the earth, yet its citizens are among the world's most fearful' (Crosby 2008:50). What is at stake is injustice inherent in the capitalistic system championed by the United States of America. 'Today we are simply told that the Empire decides for all of us and that the Empire knows what is best for us and that the highest priority of all times is "American interests"' (Nolan 2007:31). The feeling of insecurity flows logically as Colin Dueck's study of American foreign policy has shown, 'Americans tend to favour military action "either for liberal reasons, or not at all"' (Cavanaugh

2011:179). In his World Peace message on January 1, 1972, Pope Paul VI offered the oft - quoted observation that, "if you want peace, work for justice." As a critique of the condition of world poverty in the 1970, he has offered social justice as an antidote for revolutionary political movements. Timothy Raddcliffe, OP asserts, 'in the West we are more protected from illness, violence and poverty, and yet we are afraid. We are anxious about dangers that we have created' (Raddcliffe 2005:70).

Head of State living Modestly

The Head of the Vatican State differs with many government chiefs. The Pope lives in a very modest manner. During his trips abroad while the secular leaders are entitled to sleep in first class hotels like *the Sheraton*, the *Hilton*, the *Movenpick* and such comfortable locations, the Pope retreats to the Nunciature. He is hosted by the Apostolic Nunciature accredited to the particular country. Head of nation states prefer five stars hotels as suitable and dignified locations where they can meet high ranking business men and women, representative of major companies to convince them to invest in their countries, among other things. The Pope has no business agenda. In the age of globalization, many head of states follow the whims of capitalism. The Vatican state on its part has always been very sceptical of capitalism, and she has developed her social teaching in response to the social challenges facing the global community today.

Secular powers work on the basis of economic prosperity and power which always contradicts with the way Vatican conceive the duty it has in the governance of the Church. The presidents of the secular world have their own parameters, and the Pope has his own. 'The Pope is a mediator for Catholics between the secular and spiritual worlds, while the United States is a society predicated in many ways on a strict separation between state and the Church...they do offer the world very different prescriptions for achieving social, economic, political, and moral justice' (Heyer et al. 2008:202).

The Pope does not have a lucrative monthly salary which other heads of states receive. The Carmelengo, the Cardinal responsible with the papal household ensures that the Holy Father has all important basic needs. The Roman Pontiff commits his life for the Church which has become his family. His modest spending is evident for example on the means of transport he uses to make pastoral and state visits abroad. Usually head of nation states have private state owned jets. The Pope does not own a private jet but travels on commercial airlines. During his visits abroad he departs Rome on *Alitalia* and an airline from that country he is visiting usually brings him home. Unlike some head of the states who are blamed for soliciting government funds for their families and for personal use. In some African countries for example, heads of states have been blamed for procuring most expensive presidential jets which have turned to be an albatross to their own tax payers. The Pope gives all what he receives to the Church. The royalties which the Pope gets from his bestselling books are given to the Church. In his own words Pope Benedict XVI affirms; 'Not for me personally, but so that I can help others with it. And I also find it very moving that simple people enclose something and tell me, "I know that you have to help so much, and I want to do a little, too." In this respect there are all kinds of consolations' (Benedict 2010:30).

7

Global Youth Shockwaves

In this chapter we deal with an important issue about young people in society. Youth through adolescence is the most active stage in human life. It is at this stage of life when world records are won, academic achievements are registered, life engagements and enduring life friendships are forged. As such young people may prove to be very instrumental in vitalizing any society, but when left without attention, the youth out of desperation may easily become destructive.

The sub title of this book describes the world today as violent and rebellious. This is a reality as one looks at contemporary uprisings of the youth in Europe and the Middle East, and especially at the violent demonstrations and protests against world leaders. The G-8 meetings are usually accompanied by the clash between riot police and demonstrators, and some of the clashes are so severe that they cause bloodshed. There is a global rebellion of young people against the head of states and autocratic leadership. The new climate of rebellion raises concern about the security of heads of states, and in this case the Pope as the head of the State as well. We now look at what has been behind these protests and what the Church is doing.

Youth Uprising and Security Concern

In recent years, the world has been following with dismay the wide spread rebellion by youth against states, in many countries from Europe to other parts in the world. This has been prompted by the frustration caused by the way the governments forget young people and plunge them into the state of hopelessness.

Volcanic Youth Turbulence in France (2005)

The uprising of the youth in North Africa and the Arab world has dominated the media coverage for months now. This has resulted in forgetting that the unrest started in Europe. Now it is extending to other parts of the world. In France, as in the Arab world, the young people direct their anger toward politicians. One should recall that during the presidential election in 2002, which resulted into Jacques Chirac's re-election, the right-wing politician, Jean-Marie Le Pen, caused anger among Muslim immigrants due to his anti-foreigners campaign that won him second place in the results of the election, behind Jacques Chirac. His address to the French public which turned out to listen to his election campaigns were unapologetically anti-Muslim (see Juergensmeyer 2008:169).

In February 2004, France adopted a law which did not allow citizens to wear ostentatious religious symbols in public schools. The country banned "conspicuous religious symbols" in public places. The law arbitrarily forbade the nationals to display large jewellery crosses and Jewish skullcaps in court rooms, administration and other government buildings, as well as in institutes of learning. As to the Muslim families, the law was taken negatively as aiming at the Muslim schoolgirls from wearing *hijab*. The subsequent debate centred on the wearing of headscarf (or *hijab*) by Muslim girls, although it also extends to Sikh boys who have been asked not to wear turbans.

The controversy surrounding these religious symbols strikes at the heart of the dilemma for the French government of trying to integrate religious populations into secular society. Many Muslim young people of Maghreb originate from Morocco, Algeria, and Tunisia felt discriminated against and had less opportunity for jobs. The basis for this complain is that for the new generation of Maghreb women born in France and who have attended French schools, many of them wear these religious symbols out of their own free will. They have the option to wear headscarf for example, not because the fathers, husbands, male friends or even religious leaders have told them to do so. Many of them seek to express their idea of being emancipated, of being a new generation of women who make their own decision about what to wear and how to present themselves in public. Given such situation, a simply banning of religious symbols may be seen as denying women their right to free will and choice.

The grievances of the youth erupted in France in 2005. There was a nationwide rioting by African and Arab youth in cities like Marseilles, Montpellier, Lyon, etc, where tyres were burned, shops destroyed, and cars set on fire. The week long turmoil shook the French community, and unveiled the tension which existed between different communities. Young people, angry at French Authorities demolished public buildings and cars. At the heart of the matter was the displeasure of young people of foreign origin. Some chose to express their differing views on the prohibition on wearing *hijab* at school, and others blamed the government. They felt the government was not committed to provide them with a bright future. Then there is discontent with the incident of police brutality. 'Two Muslim youth were chased by police and took refuge in an electric power station, where they were accidentally electrocuted. In twenty nights of fiery protests, almost nine thousand cars were burned' (Juergensmeyer 2008:169). Widespread youth riots challenged the government with a loud voice. It helped to act as an alarm for politicians to change their attitude about immigrants.

Tunisian Eruption in (January, 2011)

The Middle East, in January of 2011 was overcome by a wave of youth revolts. The public rally for reform and democracy came to their autocratic leaders by surprise. The uprising which began in Tunisia expanded throughout the North African region, and spread to Yemen, Kuwait and Syria. We shall limit ourselves to Tunisia and Egypt, for lack of space and on relying on the information we have.

The Tunisian upheaval was a spontaneous uprising by the people, not sparked by any political leader or movement. What the world and Tunisia witnessed in January was a rebellion in a true sense and an evolution in a strict sense. It began by a public testimony, a demonstration of courage by a young man who was locally known as Basboosa, whose Islamic name is Mohamed Bouazizi a 26-year-old. He was an unemployed graduate, from a small town of Sidi Bouzid in central Tunisia. Since finding jobs was difficult, the temptation was to join other young people to cross over Europe and try to find his luck there. Every year, thousands of young people try to cross the Mediterranean to southern Europe in pursuit of a better life. It should be recounted that even in the aftermath of the uprising nearly 5000 young Tunisians, among them secondary school students, arrived on the Italian island, Lampedusa. There are around 10 million people in Tunisia and over half of them are under the age of 25. But despite having one of the most developed education systems in North Africa, unemployment is over 30 per cent and even university graduates are unemployed.

Mohamed Bouazizi overcame the temptation to risk his life in the Mediterranean Sea. He decided to remain home. He had taken to the streets with a wheelbarrow to sell fruit. As the main breadwinner of his extended family he supported his relatives and the parents. It was not easy to do this job. He was regularly stopped by the police who expected him to advance, the *bakshishi* (a small token of gratitude), in this case, however, this is bribery. But when the police trashed his wheelbarrow completely blocking his way to sell vegetables, the humiliation proved too much. The frustrated and desperate young man made his final resolution. He went to the mayor's office with a can of petrol and set fire to himself. It was an extraordinary personal act that presented the collective frustration and anger of the Tunisian masses. The death of Mohamed Bouazizi prompted nationwide protests.

This reaction follows from the harsh reality the people of Tunisia have lived during the past years. Under Ben Ali, Tunisia enjoyed a good reputation at the international scene. The country was one of the trusted allies of the United States against terrorism in the region, and European tourists chose its coastal area for holidays. But behind this good image, internally people suffered torture, oppression, censorship and corruption. The president Ben Ali and his wife kept amassing wealth. As the family of the president epitomized the power to themselves, it proved difficult to relinquish it. Therefore, from this North African country's uprising; a revolution has to come to bring something new out of it. The disgraced President was eventually forced to flee the country. He ruled his people with fear.

By fleeing abroad and because of the fall of his government, the wall of silence in Tunisia that suppressed the freedom of expression in general and in the internet in particular crumbled. After four weeks of rioting and 66 deaths, on the evening of 13th January President Ben Ali declared "I have understood you." He announced the lifting of all forms of censorship, including of the web, before explaining that he did intend to present himself in the elections of 2014. As the uprising of the youth continued to maintain its grip, the young people who organized Bloggers and other cyber-activists who were previously arrested by the police force, were released, before the President and his family left the country for exile into Saud Arabia.

Egyptian Quagmire in (January 2011)

The Egyptian rebellion as compared to the Tunisian one shed more blood before forcing the long reigning President Mubarak to vacate his post as head of the state. The rebellion in Egypt happened for two separate reasons. Firstly it was the classic failure of the political system to deal with the political, economic and social grievances of the people. The leadership was arrogant and delusional seeing only what it wanted to see and excluding anything else. The government did not take seriously people's interests, and the grievances they had. The second reason is on how it treated young people. In a country where half of the population is under the age of 30, it seemed that everything was being run by people over 65. The age gap and the inability of the system to listen to the youth and incorporate their concerns and visions angered them.

What the civilians witnessed as Mubarak designed and maintained his aristocratic rule, the rich got richer, the elite got more westernized, and the poor Egyptians, who constituted over 90% of the population, got poorer and more desperate as their living standards declined and job prospects disappeared. The Westernization of its economy and its political elite ultimately and inevitably led to the militant Islamist backlash. With political Islam, key demands for economic emancipation and social justice rose to the fore. The Coptic Christian minority who constitute 20% of the population became also a target of constant attacks by frustrated Muslim youth. Many of them were forced to flee into exile, preferring to move to those countries, such as US, Canada, and Australia where the Coptic communities expressed solidarity with the Egyptian revolution.

The Egyptian security apparatus and police force were brutal to those who opposed the Mubarak regime. Impoverished Muslims were subjected to the most brutal repression. Militant Muslims were imprisoned and tortured in the name of the US-led War against terror. The youth of the country, Muslims and Christians, were becoming increasingly frustrated with their lot. Unemployment, poverty, lack of basic educational facilities and health care enraged the masses.

It is against this dismal backdrop that the young people decided to go to the *Tahrir* square, at the centre of Cairo, to protest and rebel against repressive orders of the State. This square became the epicentre of Egypt's demonstration. Meanwhile protestors vied with and attacked the central police station and the ministry of internal affairs, including the central prison. These structures were targeted because they symbolized the cruelty and the brutal treatment of the State of its citizens. The youth in *Tahrir* square defiantly were inspired by the slogan, "civic, civic, neither military nor religious" which reads in Arabic as, "*Madaniya, madaniya, la askariya wala diniya*). In Egypt many Muslims are secular and want to see a complete separation of religion from state. Religion is a private matter, they argue, and must not be an overriding factor in the political affairs of the country. Islam has been regarded as an official religion of Egypt and the basis of legal system. Islamic *sharia* laws are deemed as the main focal point of the judicial system. Identity cards denote the religion of every

Egyptian citizen. In practice religious freedom is not provided to the citizens.

The Egyptian revolution like that of Tunisia has ushered new in hope. It is symbolic that the current people's power revolutions of North Africa are being described in flowery terms: the *Jasmine Revolution of Tunisia* and the *Lotus Revolution of Egypt*. It signals the wish of the people for more freedom, dignity and democracy.

Global Protests: Rebellion from Below

The youth rebellion today as we have learnt from the examples of the Arab world, exhibits typically a discontent and a concern of the lower class in society. This is not unrest from those with high offices and great world companies, but it is a furious rage of jobless people and the poor at the margins. It is an anger directed at political elites. We notice that most of the demonstrations and the protests which take place in the world today is globalization from below (see Nolan 2007:35). These are protests organized to express dissatisfaction against the heads of states. The first of these protests to attract the media attention took place in Seattle in 1999. Some sixty thousand representatives of a great variety of organizations marched in Seattle (USA), where one of the organs of globalization, the World Trade Organization (WTO), was meeting that year. The protest organized for this event, turned violent (see Nolan 2007:34).

Demonstrations and clashes with the police force against demonstrators have became common in G-8 meetings which have taken place in the towns like Genoa (Italy) in 2001, Davos (Switzerland) in 2005, and Heiligendam (Germany) in 2007. Due to their violent nature, these protests have forced the head of the states of the most industrialized world to meet under a tight security, and sometimes in secluded places. Most of the people who join these protests are young people. Why do these young people demonstrate and in often cases violently? What leads them to frustration? What is at stake at the international scene?

Anger at Unfulfilled Promises

It is clear that staging a peaceful demonstration is a legitimate right and an expression of that right as well. In today's world there are symptoms in many places that people have lost hope. In the families, at working places, in schools there are signs of anger everywhere. Husbands are angry in the way their wives claim self autonomy without limits. The wives too react to the way their husbands claim to be head of the family. Teachers are angered by their pupils for their demands to be treated like partners and not subjects. Everywhere, a tension of such kind exists. This shows itself on the faces of many people.

According to St. Augustine, 'hope has two beautiful daughters. Their names are anger and courage; anger at the way things are, and courage to see that they do not remain the way they are' (Odell Korgen 2007:9). We have to take St. Augustine at his words which were written later in his life, as he was a mature theologian and philosopher. By anger he did not mean that protestors should start commotion to pursue their goal through aggression. The word "anger" as used by him was meant a rational reaction duly developed as an outcome of critical observation to the contradictions which institutionally operate to discriminate, oppress and exploit the human person. This is the anger that characterizes our contemporary society. It is directed to the head of states especially those of the most industrialized nations. Taking into account the miseries currently convulsing, protestors seem determined to have their voice heard by the heads of states.

The primary cause for demonstrations and opposition to G-8 meetings is grounded on the failure to fulfil promises made in the previous meetings. The rhetoric of the decision makers bear a lot of promises for packages to the poor. After natural and human-caused disasters, donor conferences are organized, and solidarity pronouncements are issued, but in a long run the large checks seldom are released to those in a dire need. If one closely follows the pledges made during the G 8 at Gleneagles in 2005, the world's richest countries promised to spend an additional $ 50 billion per year on foreign assistance by 2010, with half that amount going to Africa. However, according to the report from the organization for Economic Cooperation and Development, foreign aid has remained stagnant despite the promise. Demonstrators are pushing for resolutions to be put into action. They intend through demonstrations to remind G-8 leaders of their moral obligation to promises.

Anger for Not Taking the Poor Seriously

There is an experience of frustration not only among the ordinary people, but also among intellectuals. Demonstrations and protests against the rich West seem to be an apocalyptic event, an eruptive cry for justice. In 2008 there was a mounting civil unrest due to rising food prices which fuelled global discontent with the fact that basic food is not reaching hundreds of millions of people around the world each year. Cardinal Christoph Schönborn of Vienna, in his weekly column series entitled *"Antwort* – the Answer" in the *Heute* Newspaper (May 2008), asks a very relevant question in face of the rising food price in the world. For him, it is a paradox that the price of bread in which the poor rely for survival should rise tremendously. This is done with no concern to children of the poor families who risks malnutrition. What is ironic is that, items like pornographic magazines that seek to serve a meagre group in society have relatively low prices. 'Given the massive amount of human suffering that goes on daily due to hunger and malnutrition, often unnoticed by the world's more well-off, the global food system is in desperate need of the same attention we give to other human rights issues as genocide and terrorism' (Schanbacher 2010: ix). Rising food prices disproportionately affect the world's poor citizens- the World Bank estimates that as many as 100 million people will be severely affected by high price of food.

The concern of the Cardinal is also shared by the Jesuit theologian Jon Sobrino who lays criticism on the savage capitalism of the West as regards professional sports, he writes, '...But the three best- paid soccer players in the world- an Englishman, a Frenchman, and a Brazilian, who all play on the same Spanish team- earn $42 million a year; by comparison to San Salvador metropolitan area, with 1,821,532 inhabitants, has an annual budget of $ 45.6 million. This is comparative harm, a shameless insult to the poor, a failure of the human family' (Sobrino 2008:26).

It is painful to consider that of the world's 6.5 billion inhabitants, the three richest persons have more assets than the combined GNP of the poorest 48 nations, a quarter of the world's countries. Annual expenditures between 2003 and 2005 indicate that the rich families spend as much money on fragrances. The rich spends more for toys and games than the poorest one-fifth of the world population earns per year. The huge spending for military operations seems to have no place in human conscience. In such deplorable situation facing the huge masses that live in extreme poverty, moral ethics challenge the conscience of the rich. "Those with worldly power must remember their spiritual and moral powerlessness apart from Christ, and those without worldly power must remember the spiritual and moral power they are given by Christ' (Ott: Netland 2008:249).

Challenging global issues on social and economic planes caution humanity against forgetting the poor. Without the prophetic stance the capitalistic global system will continue to damage the beauty of the human person. The resistance of the poor is a desire to survive. Activists demonstrate their protest against the attitude of the great nations to undermine their commitment to global solidarity. Those demonstrating in streets are appalled by the way things are. In a world of competition and profit accumulation, the world looks like "a global jungle" where the survival of the fittest is pronounced, and that might is right. In fact without an adequate vision that targets the poor and their sufferings, it is easy to lose sight of our interconnection.

The Pope: Father and Friend of Young People

The rebellion orchestrated by the frustrated youth run out of control, as the young people are determined to sacrifice their lives for change. They are tired of living in the systems that deprive them the chance to contribute to the development of their nation states. This causes us to worry about the security of the head of states. When one sees how things are unfolding in the Church, the situation is quite different. The Pope is seen by many young people as *Father* and a *Friend* (see Schönborn 2011:5).

Local Churches at the Service of Young People

In the Church young people do not feel that they are neglected nor do they feel marginalized. Young people are active and have opportunity to contribute for the growth of the Church. In all the parishes there are activities which involve the young people. The assistant Parish priests mainly are providing spiritual assistance to the youth of the parishes. The youth have a referral team of patrons/matrons whom they can rely for counselling and advice. In the parishes, young people take part in the choir, in reading the lectionaries during the holy Masses. They are also engaged in lay apostolate. Some parishes organize camping for young people during holidays where they are accompanied by the patrons. Young people are also present in the administration of the Parish, as some of the youth representatives are elected members on the Parish Council. Through these representatives the parishes and Parish priests can understand what the young people need and consider important for them. In the West, especially in Germany, Austria, Belgian and the United Kingdom, the Mass for the youth in the parishes are a moment of great enthusiasm. The young inject life and hope in the Church.

At the Diocesan level, the young people are also active. In every diocese there is a diocesan officer who is in charge of youth affairs. During Palm Sunday, which usually is a day for young people the diocesan bishops celebrate mass with young people. In parishes and diocese activities are organized by young people to remember the triumph entry of Jesus in Jerusalem. There are some dioceses which organize inter-diocesan sports competition in different parishes, thus getting young people to know each other and forge friendship among them.

Dynamism of World Youth Day

At the global level too, the youth are brought together to live the Church communion. There are two initiatives which the Church has taken for young people. The first one and this is mostly recently, is the publication of the *Catholic Church Youth Catechism*, the *Youcat*. This is the brainchild of the Austrian Cardinal Christoph Schönborn, OP in collaboration with the Austrian Bishop's Conference. The Cardinal drawing his experience from the magisterial work of preparing the *Catechism of the Catholic Church* as a Secretary of the Committee some years ago, then under the chairmanship of the present Pope, then as Cardinal Prefect; has given young people a wonderful doctrinal tool. The *Youcat* is written in a language which young people can understand. It raises questions which spring from the daily concerns of the youth. It consists of visual aids and photo images which enable young people to reflect much of what they have read. The initiative like this is one of the pastoral geniuses of our time.

This second gigantic innovation is by the late John Paul II of the *World Youth Day*. The Church follows with interest and the aspirations of young people. It is from the pastoral concern for young people that the World Youth Day was born. In the early 1980s in Rome, a group of young people in the streets just near St. Peter's Basilica met for prayers and exchange of ideas. Pope John Paul II had known this group through the information shared to him by Gerrardo Paul-Josef Cordes the Vice-President of the Pontifical Council for Laity. The idea came to the Pope to invite them and other young people around the world to celebrate the exceptional

Holy year of Redemption in 1983/84, marking the anniversary of the death of Jesus Christ.

The invitation Pope John Paul II made in 1984, for young people was received with great interest. God had graced the occasion in different ways. First, the major concern of the organisers was how to accommodate all the young people in Rome. It was decided that a gigantic tent site be constructed for the guests. Although, the city mayor of Rome wrote to reject the planned construction, the Christian spirit of hospitality prevailed. Another option was sought. This moved about 6,000 families which were mobilized in Rome, and volunteered to accommodate young people in their own houses. The stress for accommodation was overcome. The event was graced by the presence of famous personalities in the Church, who joined the young people in Rome including Mother Teresa from Calcutta, and Frère Roger, the founder of the Taizé community. There were about 300,000 young people from all over the world. A week after the youth meeting in Rome, the Pope officially inaugurated the *World Youth Day*. The institution of this event coincided with the United Nations celebration of the International Year of the Youth in 2006. The first International WYDs was celebrated in Rome in 1986. There have been 11 international World Youth Days, where the youth continue to answer the invitation of the Holy Father in staggering numbers and carry home the message received there to be Christ's light to the world.

The week-long event is filled with prayer service, Masses, catechetical sessions and concerts. Many young people see this opportunity as moment for conversion and to begin a new way of life witnessing for Christ. There is an air of mutual friendship as young people from all countries meet together to express their common faith. The WYD are graced with the presence of the Holy Father. As young people discuss with the Pope, eat food with him, listen to his catechesis, and attend his Pontifical masses, the young people discover that the Church is not something of the past, a kind of museum with an outdated moral codes but it is first of all a community of faith to which they belong. They see in the Pope not in the first place as a head of state, not as someone who comes to impose and enforce moral doctrine, but a pastor and friend. They love him and are committed to ensuring his security. This is evident for example during the *World Youth Day* at the Great Jubilee Year 2000 in the *Tor Vergata* in Rome. There were about two million young people who had gathered there. The town mayor was astonished that during the week long gathering of young people in the city there were no acts of vandalism which were reported.

During the vigil at the *Tor Vergata* in the evening Pope John Paul II was seated with many young people. Suddenly one young man crossed over the podium. He was running very quickly in such a way that the security officers could not see him. From the Television screen the young people could see the man advancing towards the Pope, and worried that he could harm the Pope, they rushed all of the sudden to form the shield to protect the Pope and no harm was done (see Schönborn 2011:5). This isolated event cannot dismiss the memory of the divine power present at the event. One remembers the salient line of young people from nearly every nation. In the Jubilee Year 2000, hundreds of thousands passed through the Holy Door of St. Peter's Basilica and got ready to receive the Sacrament of Reconciliation. The World Youth Day proves to bring much fruit and hope for the future. For many Catholics, including Pope Benedict XVI himself, World Youth Day is considered a tool of the Holy Spirit to promote Church vocations of priesthood and religious life. It is noteworthy to reproduce the words of the Pope himself:

...I cannot help saying: Something is happening here, and we are absolutely not the ones who are making it happen. In Australia, they had predicted huge security problems, difficulties and clashes, all the sorts of things that typically happen with mass demonstrations. When it was all over, the police were enthusiastic, everyone was happy, because there had been absolutely no trouble at all...And Sydney continues to bear fruit, for example, in priestly vocations. In the World Youth Days we have, I think, hit upon something that helps everyone (Benedict 2010:109).

The incidents narrated above one from Rome as witnessed by the Austrian Cardinal Christoph Schönbonn, OP and the impression which Pope Benedict had in Australia show that the young people see the Pope and the bishops as leaders of the Church in a different way they see the secular leaders.

In the Church young people are like in the family where they are active participants. The Church calendar honours some young people who have lived a saintly life. It also includes saintly pastors who should be emulated for their dedication in the pastoral care of young people like St. John Bosco and Jean Maria Vianney. Concretely in the life of the Church, Religious Congregations like the Salesian brothers and fathers, place as the priority of their charisma; the care of young people. Looking closely and objectively in the liturgical and the pastoral life of the Church, one can affirm without hesitation that the Church is a safe home for young people. Everywhere, at schools, at holidays, at working places and in families, the Church is present to offers young people answers for their spiritual and physical welfare. This is contrary to what the media represents the Catholic Church in the world based on selective cases. In fact the Church is a refuge to young people who strive for holiness, especially those haunted by sin

There are many stories of the Church offering healing for young people. In Tony Hendra's best-selling memoir, *Father Joe*, the widely known author and satirist recounts his remarkable relationship with an English Benedictine monk who, Hendra says, "saved his soul." After being caught in sexual relationship with a married woman at the age of fourteen, Tony was sent off, to see Fr. Joe at Quarr Abbey on the Isle of Wight, off the coast of England. The boy thought he was for it for sure. But instead of recriminations and guilt trips, the priest offered Tony a chance to think about a serious mistake and his own selfishness. Hendra describes an overwhelming sense of peace that he experienced as this somewhat funny-priest with floppy ears and rubbery lips offered him forgiveness (see Wallace, CSsR 2006:178).

The Church never abandons young people. She offers a systematic apostolate designed for the youth. Priests' chaplains in every parishes and Church institutions are always at their disposal to listen and guide them. In most Episcopal conferences, a Bishop is named to be a national coordinator of youth apostolate. In addition, there are religious women and men who also take part in the pastoral work among young people offering them a genuine friendship and care. They discover that the leaders of the Church try their level best to accompany young people in their day to day lives. Youth chaplains provide religious instruction in schools, celebrate Mass with young people and take part in sports and music with them. Religious sisters teach in schools and provide medication to young people in Church owned clinics and hospitals. Religious Brothers work closely with young people in schools and vocation centres. In camping with young people bishops and priests eat what the young people themselves prepare, and sleep in tents sharing the same conditions which the young people endure themselves. This makes a deep impression that the Church is not to be seen from above but is a community of love and friendship. It helps to dispel the kind of rebellion and protests which characterize the secular world today.

A Relevant Formation Required

At this era of mistrust, reprisal and bloodshed, the Church should invent adapted pastoral programme for peace. Church communities have to take seriously the background from which teenagers and young people grow up. Many families today supply to their kids all sorts of items which children demand including gun toys. Children seem to be at the happiest and safest mood when they know how to shoot and play with gun and pistol toys. The market economy promotes best selling films dominated by hero fighters who after shooting and killing their opponents are turned into celebrities. Modern film industry privileges violence and sex. The savage capitalism preaches to young people what can be termed as "unholy trinity," based on privatization, liberalization and relativism. Young people are made to believe that through their own efforts they can get what they want. Their lives are secure depending on how much they own.

In the context of a capitalistic economy, tourism industry is boosted today among other things. One way to practice leisure for many tourists travelling to sub-Saharan Africa is the hunting of animals. African hunting *safaris* have become spectacular. Violence against wild animals is recorded to rise through legal or illegal poaching. The hunting for elephants, rhinoceros, buffalos etc is encouraged by exotic films about wild Africa. The inherited tradition to hunt animals as source of food is overshadowed by a new culture which considers hunting to kill a nice hobby. It is killing animals for pleasure. Gun shots in wild life reserves violate the harmony of the jungle. The hunting *safari* augments the impression to young people that killing with a gun could become a matter of pleasure.

Besides that, the situation of insecurity in daily lives encourages young people to feel safe with the gun. What is evident today in many countries of the global South is the failure of some nation states to protect its citizens. In a situation where the state security enforcement mechanism is crippled by malfunctioning, the security market opens to non-state actors. There are many shops which sell ammunition; for which individual citizens are allowed to possess guns and pistols for their security at home. In regions where corruption is rampant, private security companies conquer the stage to offer security service to families and institutions capable to pay for the security provided. In the absence of a sanctioning authority, the private security sector is likely to enrich itself and to aggravate violence. In many places, the security companies are recognized as experts at gun shots with the intention to terrify thieves and intruders. Young people in this situation are trained to think that the gun has it all. Thus one of the compelling pastoral demand for the Church is to guide modern society not to be preoccupied much about the security of 'bodily integrity, of financial assets, of private or intellectual property, of neighbourhoods, of national boarders – to the detriment of interdependence, mutual trust, and relationship with others' (O' Connel 2009:19).

Some political discourses distort the welfare of young people. During electoral campaigns some politicians warn their citizens about insecurity brought by the presence of immigrants. Migrants have been addressed as "criminals" and as "economic competitors." As a result the narratives about "foreigners" have predominantly ascribed them with negative image of being security breakers. In many Western communities today there is an 'immigration security dilemma' (Alexseev 2011:511). The immigration security dilemma posits on uncertainties and mistrust to migrants and refugees. The natives must possess guns to ensure security against unknown strangers.

Unfortunately, the obsession with security spearheads an uncritical sense of nationalism. The preoccupation is to guarantee security to nationals, which tends to channel resources and finances towards militarization instead of doing justice to the poor. The preoccupation with armed protection to combat the "mistrusted" stranger fuels the passion for resorting to the use of gun by the young generation.

It is for this situation the Church should invent appropriate pastoral programmes for the youth. And this is to help them be aware of the need to avoid violence. The Church is the icon of the Holy Trinity. She transmits to those who believe in God, a life in full. It is a life that originates from the Father, in the Son and the Holy Spirit. Young people should neither put trust in the possession of a gun, nor in its use. Since dispensing of justice and peace are twinned, young people need to be informed to uphold justice and the love of the neighbour. In schools, recreational centres, and religious functions, they should be helped to live as children of God. They should be informed on the importance of reconciliation and forgiveness. Parents, teachers and the guardians should be critical of the policy of guns. The inner peace is acquired essentially by being freed from the yokes of sin.

8

A Moral Pitfall of Nation States

This is the last chapter of this book. From the previous seven chapters, we have shown that the protection of the person of the Pope is a matter calling for our fresh attention. The situation in the secular world has changed dramatically. People are impatient with challenges of life and tend to be violent. Some nation states sponsor violence. We read news of secret agents using false passports and fake identities to accomplish missions of killing targeted enemies abroad. The elimination of selected individuals is done not only by the security personnel, but also through snipping, car bombing, aerial attacks, and remote controlled drone strikes.

Unfortunately, in the past the social teaching of the Church has not addressed the security institutions like the *CIA* (USA), the *KGB* (Russia), Israel's national intelligence agency the *Mossad*, the *Interpol* among others directly. All these institutions have not been treated in view of on how they violate human rights and on how they overlook a shared responsibility to safeguard human life. Assassinations and targeted killings by agents of security institutions have involved clandestine operations. There are moral and pastoral problems with such kinds of operations. At a moral level any human being has a right to be treated fairly and to get listened. This requires that those declared "enemies" of states should be apprehended and an opportunity for judicial procedures be afforded them. It is also a pastoral concern, because every Christian believer and members of other religions have the right to get spiritual assistances from respective pastors before they face executions. We think that assassinating targeted persons in a manner that denies them legal procedures is a kind of political violence. In the same way, from a pastoral point of view we think that to execute someone before he/she receives spiritual support from church minister, is psychologically torturing and no doubt it is spiritual violence. In fact such executions risk the states, to abuse the very human rights which statesmen vow to protect. We intend in this chapter to emphasize that the disciples of Jesus Christ must strive to make a difference. We need to think differently and act differently.

In the previous chapters we have shown that while the security of the Pope needs to be strengthened, that should not be done in such a way as to prevent the Pope from doing his pastoral work. He is a pastor and head of state but not in the manner of nation - states. Any attempt to protect the person of the Holy Father should be done with the understanding that, the Church has entrusted the Pope to the protection of Mary, the Virgin Mother of God and St. Joseph her spouse. One of the significant achievements reached by Catholic artists is to have presented Mary, the new Eve as protector of all who seek refuge to her. In one of the paintings, the Virgin Mary is shown to wear a huge mantel in which the faithful are accommodated for safety. The Church believes also in the existence of the guardian angels. They too are responsible in protecting the Pope. We have learned from the Book of the Acts of Apostles quoted in this book, the fact that St. Peter himself was set free by guardian angels from unjust imprisonment.

We seek to insist in this chapter that the provision of security as supported in security discourses of modern nation states may be misleading. The word *security* is not synonymous with the word *peace*. Peace is more than a mere understanding of life without fear from an external enemy. Peace entails justice, the attitude of a harmonious relationship with other human beings. It is a peaceful co-existence between nations, a just extraction of the natural resources and a responsible care for creation. It is to be regretted that many nation states especially those of the West combat terrorism through military operations; thus prompting extremists to respond in the same manner, 'Christians must stand out from the rest of society' (Garrity Ranaghan 2011:69). Gerhard Lohfink is worried that, 'western...Christians are no longer aware that the church as a whole should be an alternative type of society' (Lohfink 1984:124). It is for

Christians in view of their baptismal call to live as children of God. The Eucharistic sharing invites them to communion with God and the rest of humanity. For this matter, the Christians must testify that forgiveness and love are gateways to the transformation of humanity not violence.

We intend in this chapter also to highlight that a retaliatory warfare with the aim to punish enemies and impart "a clear message" to them especially when it is done by the West do harm the image of Christianity. The West is considered to be Christian and to be guided by Christian values. Pope Benedict XVI at the beginning of his reign in 2005 abandoned the title "Patriarch of the West." The title was discarded because the Roman Catholic Church is now a global institution. The Catholic faithful are found in the West as well as in the East, in former states where only Orthodox Christians were permitted in the past, and in the global South. The title "the Patriarch of the West" overshadows this reality.

The abandoning of the title compromises in a better way with the new face of the Church, which has its majority faithful in places of extreme poverty. 'Poverty in the world today is not simply misfortune, bad luck, or inevitable-the result of laziness or ignorance or a lack of development. Poverty in the world today is the direct result of the political and economic policies of governments, political parties, and big business' (Nolan 2008:39). It is a result of the moral pitfall of the political order. The many Catholics who live in Latin America, Asia and Africa unlike their brothers and sisters in the West are in places without material richness, and for that are away from the part of the world which influences major decisions of the world. The title "the Patriarch of the West" in a certain sense implies that the Pope protects the status quo of the richest region over other regions of the globe, its cultural and theological hegemony and all what this implies. Reading carefully the signs of the times as to what the Holy Spirit speaks to the churches, the abandoning of the title seems to be providential.

Taking the global character of Catholicism into consideration, we are going to challenge the nation states for pursuing extreme nationalistic policies which marginalize and sometimes demonize foreigners who do not have citizenship and those from other religious backgrounds. This is true in the West as is in Arabic countries and in some Asian and African countries as well. One has sadly to point out that: where as religious freedom, for example has been embraced widely in Christian countries after World War II to the present time, opportunities for religious freedom have diminished tremendously in Islamic countries. The real situation suggests that there is less religious freedom in Islamic countries than it was a couple of decades ago. As a result many Christians are either killed or forced to flee their countries. Where religious freedom and the respect of the minority groups are denied, the propensity towards violence is likely to be augmented. This is truly so, especially when one learns that the terrorist groups are brewed mainly from countries without religious freedom. The waves of terrorism, financial crisis, and the political unrest as the one which has swept over the Arab world shows clearly that physical security, economic stability and social safety cannot be achieved without setting the human heart aright. There is a need for conversion of the heart.

The Human Heart is what is at Stake

In view response to threat from terrorist attacks, security organs have consolidated the monitoring of the movements of people. There are check points in most important gatherings; be it in airports, in workshop meetings and in huge gatherings of people. The police employ metal detectors and scanning. Although the scanners and metal detectors are important for security; the Church sees that what is at stake is the darkness of the human heart. The human heart must be set aright. 'The terrain of the human heart is an infinitely vast mystery with limited capacity for good and for evil...Correcting the disorders in society challenges us first to understand the terrain of the human heart' (Groody 2008:10, 11).

The issues of security and peace are not inseparable with the virtues of hospitality and gentleness. The Acts of the Apostles show just that for the Christians of the early centuries of Christianity. Christian believers in the primitive Church trusted in the power and love of God. They lived in such a way that their houses were sources of community life and individual protection. The practice of hospitality, mutual forgiveness and common prayer strengthened the bond among them. These people were of one heart (see Acts . 4:32). As a community of faith, love and hope, the early Christians never surrendered to the lure of worldly style of procuring security. They never had an army or police of their own. Yet they became a strong community that won respect and admiration even from the Romans and Jews.

The spirituality of peace and simplicity of the early Church should be emulated today; to lead the Church away from "politics of power." Such politics privileges violence. The main reason why the Church should not entertain the politics of power and it tactics of violence as is the case with nation states, it is because it follows the whims of lying. "We live in a world of lies, where no one believes in anything any longer" (Sobrino 2008:111). Politicians tell lies for the purpose of showing the civilians that they care for their security. To get support from the citizens to wage wars, commanders in chiefs in some cases pronounce false and deceiving statements of what St. Augustine calls the "manifest lie" and what St. Thomas Aquinas coins as the "perfection of lying." Some statements by politicians designed to justify declaring of war 'constitutes a lie – a "duplicitous utterance" and the *de facto* are pronounced with a clear intention to deceive (see DECOSSE 2006:384). War has always been supported to feed parochial interests. Brueggemann states correctly: 'We now have abundance of false worlds constructed by the feeding frenzy of consumerism and by the national passion for exceptionalism (choseness) that feeds military adventurism and economic expansionism...The force of that ideology has compelling and coercive ways to punish those who say or act otherwise' (Brueggemann 2011:xiii). The postmodern military operations employ advanced weapons to punish certain parts of the world because of the offenses committed by few individuals. One serious concern with the proposal to punish collectively for the offenses committed by a few terrorists, for example, is that 'such a move might be based on the unfair assumption of the guilt by association. This concern is rooted in an objection to blaming and punishing the many for the misdeeds of the few.' (Erskine 2010:272).

Lies which politicians use to support wars they wage against other countries do not last long. Taking the example of the American soldiers who went to fight war in Vietnam, most of the soldiers later on decided that the war was unjust when they returned back home. A good number of them came to this conclusion in the midst of combat while in Vietnam (see Ryan 2011:34). The 1991 Gulf War experience by one particular serviceman appears to cement the same idea of unjust wars waged with propaganda of lies. The soldier states upon coming back in the USA, 'I served in the war in Kuwait,' he began, 'but I didn't want to be there, I didn't like being there, I dislike the 130 – degree temperature, and I thought being there was wrong. The war was about money, about oil, and we shouldn't have been there, and we didn't accomplish anything, because we still have the same problem' (Camp 2008:140).

In addition to what we have shown above, the justification of warfare always begins with miscalculations. At the beginning of World War I in 1914, German thought its armies would reach Paris in thirty days after mobilization. Austria thought it would snuff out the Serbs in a couple of weeks. Russia thought it would destroy the German army in East Prussia in a single battle. NATO operations in Libya projected to incapacitate the military power of Colonel Gaddafi in Libya and finally force him out of power within eighteen days. The bombardment which started in March 2011 took all the way through until August 2011 when Gaddafi was finally killed.

It should be underlined that resorting to war is a human defeat. It results in the desecration of human bodies. During warfare the human bodies are tortured, executed, and left to a state of total despotism. Captured soldiers and prisoners of war are mistreated and their dignity abused. Cardinal Francis Stafford, the former Archbishop of Denver (U.S.A) reproduces a gruesome memory of a young American soldier after the 1991 Desert Storm War. What haunted the young man after the war is his massive guilt over an action following an order to bury living Iraqi soldiers. Since they were surrendering in such large and unexpected numbers while still in their trenches, the Iraqis seemed to constitute no threat to the security of the allied forces. The young American soldier obeyed his military superior and used his bull-dozer to bury alive hundreds, possibly thousands (see Wallace, CSsR, 2006:177). War is a very dangerous affair it cannot be waged without the splitting of innocent blood. For scholars like David DECOSSE, what is common to all the modern methods of political lying is an element of violence (see (DECOSSE 2006:380). Inside political rhetoric is always the portrayal of the mighty of the nation states. This eventually credits the politicians as of admirable leadership.

The Papacy without Tiara

After suffering much from centuries of persecution in the hands of different Emperors, and following the Constantine verdict, the Church enjoyed a time of peace and calm. She steadily lost her initial centrality in the understanding of herself as a pilgrim community, and embarked to side with the worldly powers. The popes and bishops were crowned as princes and emperors. The Church became so powerful and indeed a perfect society. She began to humiliate its opponents, and resorted to the use of force and military invasions, "the crusades" in some cases, to spread the faith.

The Pope regarded himself to have secular power even to depose the Emperor. The tiara became a symbol of the Pope's secular powers. By taking alliance with worldly security paradigm, the Church neglected her very original sense of being a "little flock" that should have no fear at all. "Do not be afraid, little flock, for it is your Father's good pleasure to give you the kingdom...For where your treasure is, there your heart will be also" (Lk 12:32-34). The Church does not have to share in the anxiety of the world of piling up earthly glory, military weapons and prestige. "Diaspora" is the word Karl

Rahner used to describe the nature of the Church. In his mind, the Church really belongs to a Diaspora (see MacPherson 2008:8). In fact Christianity as global reality finds herself to be everywhere as in a Diaspora. It is for this truth that the Christians were so named not in Jerusalem but in the Diaspora, at the Greek city of Antioch.

The Papacy of Pope Paul VI abolished the wearing of the tiara in order to implement the reform of Vatican Council II. The same Pontiff also abolished the *Palatine Guard* in 1970, to strip the Papacy of military protection in the manner of the nation states. The presence of such an army is a signal of readiness to have recourse to violence. The new "culture of peace" which was the idea that came with the publication of the Pastoral Constitution *Gaudium et Spes*, made it suggested suspending the Palatine Guard. It is to be recalled that during the Second World Wars (1939-1945), particularly in September 1945 when the German troops occupied Rome, the *Palatine Guard* was given responsibilities to protect the gardens and courtyards of the Vatican City. On more than one occasion these soldiers resorted to violent confrontations with Italian Fascist police units working with the German authorities to arrest political refugees who were hiding inside the Vatican (see *Wikipedia* 2011).

To avoid confusing the papacy with the leadership models of secular world powers, Pope Benedict XVI removed the tiara image in his pontifical emblem. A reform such as this is essentially relevant for the papacy prepared to serve the wider ecumenical Church family. The World Christianity anticipates that the Pope is key player in leading Christians towards full unity. The pontificate of Benedict XVI shows a steadfast will to wear the shoes of the Galilean fisherman. The abandonment of the tiara signals the Church's departure from "provisional security" of the secular powers. From its long history the Church is aware that it is not violence which procures peace. Secular powers are temporal and are not long lasting. Cardinal Francis George of Chicago who took part in the conclave that elected Pope Benedict VI in April 2005, and was privileged to witness the Pope greeting the crowd for the first time from the Balcony of St. Peter. He narrates what passed in his mind during the occasion:

I was gazing over toward the Circus Maximus, toward the Palatine Hill where the Roman Emperors once resided and reigned and looked down upon the persecutions of Christians, and thought, "Where are their successors? Where is the successor of Caesar Augustus? Where is the successor of Marcus Aurelius? And finally, who cares? But if you want to see the successor of Peter, he is right next to me, smiling and waving at the crowds (Barron 2011:35).

The reflection of Cardinal George is insightful. The Caesars being emperors of the Romans were protected by violence. The elimination of enemies of the Empire was an institutionalized brutality of the state. In cruel competitions organized by the aristocratic class, weak opponents were summarily executed whereas the victors were honoured and accorded a state honour. The Roman Empire adored violence that humiliated its enemies and the glory of the state. Ironically, however, the Empire was ruined by the very violence it relied upon in order to survive. The lust for bloodshed by the aristocracy and the Roman soldiers, led the execution of helpless slaves and captives of war. The unmerciful behaviour of the state fuelled hate among citizens, who disliked the Empire. Internal riots and rebellion paved a way to the weakening of the state. The option for violence never protected the Roman Empire to an enduring security.

The Vatican State: Dismissing Wrong Assumptions

In Europe and America there is a "rebellion" against established institutions as we pointed at the introduction of this book. More and more people are posing questions about the legality of the Vatican State. Pope Benedict XVI visits to some parts of Europe have been greeted by sections of protestors whose claim among other things question the legitimacy of mixing religion and politics.

During Pope Benedict XVI's visit to Germany in September 2011, a dozens German opposition MPs announced plans to boycott the address the Pope was scheduled to deliver in the *Bundestag*, the lower house of parliament, in protest against the "violation of state neutrality" by the head of the Catholic Church. Several MPs of the Left Party and those belonging to the social Democratic Party (SPD) as well as those of the Ecological Green Party publicly expressed their opposition to the Pope's address the house. The rationale for their protests rested on the "wisdom" of separating the Church from getting involved in politics.

Some historians criticize the Vatican State based on the lack of international consensus. From historical analysis the creation of the Vatican State is a result of the Lateran treaty, the concordance of 1929 agreed upon between Mussolini and the Vatican. Historians contend that the concordance agreed between Mussolini and the Vatican was a unilateral deal not shared by representatives of other nation – states. For that some argue that, if this manner of the creation of the state is possible, there can be room for Great Britain for example, to declare the Anglican See of Cantebury as a State, or in Saudi Arabia to raise the pilgrimage area of Mecca, to the status of a State. They opined further that even if the Vatican lost its statehood after the Prussian war that interrupted Vatican Council I (1869-70), before it was re – established by Mussolini in 1929, to them, 'the Holy See as government of the Vatican, has an international personality that has been recognized and with which states have diplomatic relations quite apart from the matter of statehood' (Fodden 2011).

More objections against the Vatican State make reference to the Montevideo Convention on Rights and Duties of State of 26 December 1933, Article 1 which reads, 'the state as a person of international law should possess the following qualifications: (a) a permanent population, (b) a defined territory, (c) a government and (d) capacity to enter into relations with other states' (Fodden 2011). According to Fodden, 'the Vatican might have difficulty with the permanent population' (Fodden 2011).

From above it is easy to notice a misunderstanding, as it is clear that many people do not know the why the Vatican is a State. In addition, it is apparently clear that some people fail to get the point what kind of State it is. We intend in this section to shed light so as to remove such confusion.

Let us make it clear to our readers that the dispute about the relationship between the Church and the State is a perennial one (see Rahner 1992:9). The word "state" is generally used to a express a political form through which a specific group of people present themselves in a stable manner guided by precepts and prescribed laws (see Cavanaugh 2011:9). The term *status* to which the concept "state" derives began to appear in a political context only in the late fourteenth century, and up until sixteenth century. The state emerged in Europe amidst the late Renaissance and Reformation periods. The state as we know it today is a relatively new invention, originating in Europe between 1450 and 1650 (see Porter 1994:6).

It is necessary to recall that in the Constantinian era Christianity became a "State- Religion." From this time on what reigned was the dictum *cuius regio, eius religio* (the religion of the emperor is the religion of the state). The Church enjoyed both spiritual and secular powers. The spiritual movements were led by religious orders. The contemplatives, mendicants and mystics challenged the Church to abandon the worldly style of statehood and remain with its "spiritual statehood." In this development one can say that the state is an ancient institution found in all societies at a certain stage of historical development. Thus, 'the state is not a product of society, but creates society' (Cavanaugh 2011:18). The Church as a stable institution with its own manner of governance enjoys its own type of statehood.

While the Vatican State was established in 1929, the Holy See as a creature of international law is centuries old (see Collins 2011). Although the Vatican might have missed the criteria of having "permanent population" as the Montevideo convention prescribes, the Holy See has permanent observer status at the United Nations. It is treated as a state under customary international law with the completely ability to negotiate multilateral treatise as a state. What kind of the state is the Vatican?

The Vatican is Not a Nation – State

Most of the objections against the Vatican State seem to consider her as a nation-state. This is to miss the point. The nation-states as we have them today are of recent making. Many of the African countries south of the Sahara, for example, are a result of the Berlin Conference (1884-1885). In the West, many nation-states were established between 15th and 16th centuries in order to protect the rights of human family. One of the motor which catalyzed the creation of nation states is the abolition of institutionalized evils such a slave trade. The nation- states were necessary to prevent warfare which was rampant among warring ethnic groups.

As slaves were brought to freedom they had a feeling of being born anew. The Declaration of the Rights of Man promulgated in 1789 had stated clearly that the human person should have rights. The nation-states were consequently established in order to protect the rights of the human family. The state sovereignty took charge to safeguard the liberty and emancipation of her people as well as her territory. This paved a way to the concept of *nation*. This idea is derived from the Latin word *nascere* (to be born). With the abolition of the slave trade and the creation of nation-states, the word "nation" came to refer to a geographical territory from which a naturalization of its citizens is acquired by birth. In a nation-state, the rights, duties and privilege of citizens are acquired not from their free will, but naturally from the fact that one is born in the territory.

Given this historical fact, one can say that the nation-state is not something natural, taking the case of Africa for example. The Berlin Conference divided Africa into nation states as colonial masters saw it appropriate. Africans themselves were not invited to make their opinions heard. 'Most nation states have resulted from violence, the conquered territories of victors, in the cruel war for dominance and control' (O'Murchu 2008:185). This has scarred harmony between African states. The Igbo and Yoruba who are predominantly Christians, and relatively settled were forced to live with the Fulani and Hausa of the northern part of Nigeria who are predominantly

Muslim and pastoralists by lifestyle. The Makonde ethnic people extend beyond Tanzanian border to Mozambique were divided and required to live in two separate sovereign states. The same applies to *Maasai* of Kenya and Tanzania for example. The nation-states which were born from the consensus reached among imperialist powers, denied the native population the very freedom for which the nation states were created for.

Besides this historical pitfall, in their pretext to protect the citizens registered through birth, the nation states tend to be xenophobic. This complicates the status of immigrants even after naturalization. The truth is that for a nation with a majority of black people there may develop a tendency to discriminate against the white minority population even if they are born there and vice versa. Jenny Hwang an American with Korean origin shares her experience in the United States:

I was not an immigrant myself but grew up in an immigrant home. Growing up as a minority, I wondered whether people would ever just think of me as an American without having my appearance predispose them to think I was a "foreigner." In fact, in order to fit in, I didn't want to learn the Korean language growing up and struggled with whether to be proud of my Korean heritage. Even though I speak English fluently, love American football and have been educated here, people are surprised sometimes that I can speak English as well as I can, and they have often asked me "where are you really from." (Soerens: Hwang 2009: 20-21).

The etymological meaning, the word "nation" has to do with birth. This means that many people find themselves to living in states which are not of their personal choice. This reality compels us to treat immigrants with understanding. The fact that they are born in Japan, for example, does not mean that they fully accepts what the Japanese state regulates for its citizens. This fact questions the rationale of the state to demand an absolute loyalty to its citizens. This problem of the nation – state as regards the free choice of its citizens whether to belong there or not is not a problem with those who have loyalty to the Vatican State. This loyalty pertains to the faith which one has received in the Church. The Christians according to Tertullian are not born, but they are made. Usually the decision to be baptized is made out of one's free will.

From what we have developed above, the question we think some of our readers are likely to ask is why then the Church keeps the baptism of infants? As regards the infant baptism it depends on the will of the parents. They are obliged to share with their children human and spiritual values they deem significant. No responsible parent anywhere waits until the child is grown up so as to hand to the child the "mother tongue" for example. Nature has ordained that at the infancy stage, the child relies entirely on his/her parents for growth into faith and other societal values. A complete mutual trust and dependence which the child deposits to the parents, presupposes that the decision of parents to baptize their child is consented. Nothing rationally justifiable at spiritual and cultural realms which are esteemed so by the parents should jeopardize the welfare of the child. Upon reaching her adult stage, the baptized faithful must voluntarily manifest the free will of the faith received by active membership in the Church. The Gospel of John puts it, "But all who received him, who believed in his name, he gave power to become children of God" (Jn 1:12).

The Catholic Church is a composition out of the vision from the Book of Revelation, it is a conglomeration of individuals "from every nation, tribe, people, and language" (Rev. 7:9). The decision to be members of the Church is made freely, out of baptism which one registers either with the consent of parents on behalf of the child, or an adult member who has decided out of his free will to join the Church. This free will to matters of belief and moral teachings of the Church demands an accent and loyalty for individual. Some of them of them requires full accent and bind the Christian in conscience depending on what levels the teachings are placed in the hierarchy of truth. It is not biological birth and its territorial stamp which comes first, but the grace of baptism which overcomes arbitrary demarcations such as national boundaries, racial and ethnic identities. The Roman Catholic faithful worldwide do require a passport, and neither parish congregations, nor dioceses impose a "passport control" for its new comers.

The nation-state tends to protect its territorial interests thereby elevating differences among its citizens and those from other countries. It preaches "best" and "excellence" among its citizens. In doing so it amplifies the greatness of its nation states. The countrymen and women are instilled with patriotism which accentuates their national identity and calls the citizens to committed loyalty to the nation. The particular identity of nation – state goes public as the national flag is portrayed in T-shirts, official buildings, military uniforms, embassies abroad, international sports and airports, and, indeed in different ways and places. Loyalty to the nation - state is demanded even to the point of dying for the state. 'The modern nation- state, in whatever guise, is a dangerous and unmanageable institution, presenting itself on the one hand as a bureaucratic...it invites one to lay down one's life on its behalf...(I)t is like being asked to die for the telephone company' (Cavanaugh 2011:37).

In order to protect its territorial integrity, and the security of its nationals the nation states legitimize the militarization of its armed forces. Secret agents may be sent to pursue enemies of the state beyond its borders. Conquering one's enemies is considered a holy mission for the destruction of evil. This mission justifies the application of whatever violent means necessary. In order to convince its citizens that war is justified, God is invoked to support the agenda for action. Thus the Germans, in World War I, were convinced that the Almighty was on their side: *Gott mit uns* – "God with us" – or so proclaimed the inscription on the belt buckles of German soldiers. One can also draw the experience of recent American war on terrorism. After the attack on World Trade Centre, President George W. Bush identified Iraq, Iran, and North Korea as an "axis of evil," while depicting the United States as the bearer of God's light (see Camp 2008:55). 'Along with such crusade language, the president co-opted language reminiscent of Jesus' claim to ultimate allegiance: "Around the world, the nations must choose. They are with us, or they're with the terrorists'" (Camp 2008:55). In some extreme positions the nation states tend to possess God as part of the nation. An example can be taken from the remark of Lt. Gen. William Boykin, the Deputy Undersecretary of US Defense for Intelligence, that shocked many Americans outside the military, as he characterized the wars he had fought in the religious terms, stating that he was victorious over a Muslim warlord because "My God was bigger than his. I knew my God was a real God and his was an idol" (See Perabo 2010:250). That such high ranking military officer would align the Christian God with the American military, raised concerns among both Christians and non- Christians, in the United States. In fact this officer reproduced a psychology of superiority typical of a prosperous nation state. External successes may count as criteria for endorsing divine presence.

Such a mentality obliges the subjects of the nation state to show their loyalty to the state. With the rise of the nation state 'the language of martyrdom on behalf of the celestial patria had begun to shift to martyrdom on behalf of the earthly *patria*' (Cavanaugh 2011:148). In fact this is a paranoia which was born with the rise of the nation state, for no longer as the Church relinquished its political power to the secular state, the martyrdom *pro fide* was eclipsed by or included in martyrdom *pro patria*, which extolled as a work of caritas on behalf of one's countrymen (see Cavanaugh 2011:148). To this development military personnel were required to swear loyalty to die for the nation state. Soldiers were obliged to obey their commanders without questioning and take part in war as an absolute dedicates service for the country. From the time of Tertullian military service itself, was seen as source of two primary dangers: violence and idolatry. In this sense the military is an institution of the nation state which competed with the Church to become the centre of the Christian life. The Latin thinker conceived that there can be no compatibility between an oath (*sacramentum*) made to God and one made to man, this would involve giving one's soul to two masters, God and Caesar (see Perabo 2010: 253).

In modern states we see soldiers sent to the combat zones even without their moral consent but they have to obey the nation state. Going to the war zone and inflict death to enemies is an act of violence. The nation – state foster the elimination of the opponents and encourages a corporate type of Christianity. Like everything corporate, such Christianity is obsessed with order and control. It loves grandeur, money collection, public rallies, publicity, power, and more wars. The chaplains bless the servicemen and women on mission as "beloved sons and daughters" of the nation state. The tanks, artillery guns, drones and warplanes are sprinkled with holy water to succeed in their killing mission against the enemies of the state. The fallen soldiers in caskets receive a requiem mass as Christians but who are "heroes" of the patria. For the corporate Christianity, wars are the "will of God." After the dramatic death of civilians it sends money and short- term missionaries to supply food and medicine for the victims.

The danger of embracing idols of this world and drifting away from worshipping true God is all out through history of worldly powers. We are told in the Bible that the Israelites with the intention to achieve physical security approached prophet Samuel to allow them to copy a structure of governance of the nation states as was the case in Babylonia, Mesopotamia even as near as Philistine. The man of God was worried of idolatry and injustices the secular lifestyle is going to permeate among the people of God. Samuel sternly warned the people about such dangers (see 1 Sam 8:11-18) which the people refused to listen to him and pressurized the old man to yield to their demand.

In the past and it is in our days the idolatry is inherent in politics which extols the *patria*. It shifts the loyalty of the Christian faithful from allegiance to what the Church teaches towards fulfilling what the secular states proposes. In this sense religious images, including references to God, contain secular meanings. There is a big irony for a Christianity which supports an absolute allegiance to the state. The most important question is about the citizens' allegiance to the nation state: whether their allegiance is destined to worship "one God," revealed in Jesus Christ, or the national flag which represent the god of the nation state? The problem is not the allegiance itself but to what extent should the citizens obey the nation state. Taking the United States as an example, since 1947, the Supreme Court has declared about the government neutrality toward religion, but in a nation whose motto "In God We Trust" and which pledges allegiance to "One Nation under God" there is something to ponder about. The public square is not even neutral in the context of religious pluralism. Politicians resort to biblical and Christian values to justify some of their positions. But at the heart of a rapidly secularizing country, like the United States is, atheists on their part criticize the attitude of the government to apply Christian values in politics. They judge Christianity to be an enemy to neutrality which the state identity with, in order to accommodate all its citizens. This is the idea shared also by secularists; they oppose vehemently to religious imagery and all that religion represents in American politics. This is not a place to continue with this kind of debate for it is not what we seek to share with our readers. We must be focused.

The Vatican State is manifestly guided by the wisdom of the Gospel. It is a state which heralds the advent of the kingdom for which Jesus Christ is the King; the kingdom that promote the values of justice, peace and love. A Christian grows in intimate relationship with Jesus Christ by participation. Everyone is an adult, full member of the communion that lives the *diakonia* (mutual service), *marturia* (mutual Gospel life witness), *kerygma* (mutual gospel proclamation) and *litourgia* (common worship) of all members. No one of the baptized is virtually denied to live a fully Christian life. Everyone is entitled to sacramental life of the Church. Everywhere, a member of the Church of Christ meets his brothers and sisters in Christ. Hence the famous statement of St. John Chrysostom applies here 'the one who dwells in Rome knows that those in most distant parts to be his members' (see *Lumen Gentium* no. 13). In secular politics things are quite different. In nation states especially in developing countries:

Every few years people vote governments into power but really have little or no say about what happens in the intervening periods. The major decisions affecting people's lives will not be made from within these "super powers" with people's interests at stake. They will be dictated by international market forces (controlled by corporations), and those in governance have become very adept at convincing the gullible electorate that the decisions are coming from within a country when in fact they are totally dictated by forces from outside (O'Murchu 2008:186)

It is no wonder some scholars like Diarmuid O'Murchu thinks that the 'nation state has lost virtually all semblance of just and empowering governance' (O' Murchu 2008:186). Because of the failure of the nation states, O'Murchu calls for an alternative way of leading the people in a manner that is to be more *organic* (honouring the aliveness of everything in creation), *holarchical* (supporting the relational web of life), *collaborative* (endorsing cooperation rather than competition), and empowering (calling forth the mutual giftedness of all creatures) (see O' Murchu 2008: 187).

The Vatican is Not an Autocratic State

Some critical views hold that the Holy See does not have a legitimacy to be a state, and foremost it is an autocratic institution. This claim has no basis at all. The Pope is not an autocratic ruler. He is not a product of a succession from a monarchy. The Bishop of Rome is elected by the College of Cardinals. Once elected the Pope does not lead the Church in a unilateral manner but collegially. As head of the Vatican State the Pope has many assistants around him; the cardinals, bishops; monsignors and some knowledgeable lay persons.

The Holy See manages the affairs of the Church through consultations, dialogue and the seeking of opinions from responsible persons at local churches. Neither the Pope nor the cardinal prefects run the congregations and dicasteries with an "iron fist." They don't just pile up orders and commands, but are in constant contacts with their assistants. The Church as we have mentioned already is a community of free will. Obedience to authority is exercised with attentive consent and a loving disposition for the welfare of the Church. In the spirit of fraternity and responsibility; and those assigned with different duties in the Church fulfils them in collaboration with the hierarchy. The collaboration and participation of everyone in the Church is made possible, thanks to the structures of dialogue which are established from parishes to the diocesan levels. Such a community of disciples where fraternal relations are in order dismisses an autocratic type of leadership.

The Church enjoys her autonomy. She manages a government with its own style of statehood; and living side by side with the secular state she is careful not to be autocratic. She knows very well that she is answerable to God. "The earth is LORD's and all that is in it" (Ps 24:1). God is the sole ruler, Christ is the King, as the Church proclaims. With this in mind, the Church is a "theocracy" not a "democracy." When Samuel bows to the pressure of the Israelites that they live like other nations, thus anoints Saul the first king, the LORD complains that, "they have rejected me from being king over them" (1 Sam 8:7).

The recognition of God as the sovereign King of the universe has prompted some Christian communities to develop the so called: "Dominion Theology" and "Reconstruction Theology." Proponents of these theologies support and organize violence aimed to subject every human person to follow the will of God. They struggle to restore the Christian theocratic state (see Juergensmeyer 2008:183). This is a cause of concern which merit critics. The understanding of the Church as a "theocracy" is qualified, however, with the recognition that the Church herself is not God. She is made up of human beings who darken this community of faith with their personal sins and failures. The weakness of the faithful, pastors and non pastors has been a cause of scandal and sufferings. Most of these scandals in the Church have often been a direct result of abuse of power and authoritarian leadership. The historical experience of sin encourages the Church to live humbly and to do penance. Over many years the Church has struggled to overcome nostalgia of the Constantine era. This enables the Church to refrain from a crusading mind of the past. The use of violence is not a policy of the Church of Christ. Miroslav Volf cautions Christians that welding the sword "for" God is actually a veiled attempt to "be" God, preserving the fundamental difference between God and non-God, he says, is essential. 'The biblical tradition insists that there are things which only God may do; one of them is to use violence' (Volf 1996:301).

In order not to fall to an autocratic model of leadership the Church strives to observe the separation of powers. Pope Benedict XVI writes in *Deus Caritas Est*:

> the just ordering of society and the state is central responsibility of politics. Fundamental to Christianity is the distinction between what belongs to Caesar and what belongs to God (cf Mt. 22:21), in other words, the distinction between Church and state, or, as the Second Vatican Council puts it, the autonomy of the temporal sphere...For her part, the Church, as the social expression of Christian faith, has a proper independence and is structured on the basics of her faith as a community which the state must recognize. The two spheres are distinct, yet always related (Benedict XVI 2005: no. 28).

This separation of powers between the Church and the State does not mean that the Church should resign from politics. Those who criticize the Church as meddling with a field not within her competence tend to think that the Church is not in this world. In 1984 during his pastoral visit in Belgium, Blessed John Paul II met a group of enthusiastic students at Louvain – La- Neuve Catholic University who carried placards with a message, *"voie que tu fais de la politique"* meaning, "confess that you do politics." The students wanted to accuse the Pope of mixing a spiritual role and a political one.

The Church does not play a partisan political role in the world, for this belongs to the secular governments and political parties. Yet, as spiritual institution concerned with the welfare of human persons as a whole, the Church has moral obligation to be active in politics; and it is for that it can defend the rights and support genuine democratic reforms in places like Africa, Latin America, and Arabic countries.

Some politicians make objection that the Church's political stance is sectarian for it is a community of the baptized, which is a distinct group that excludes the others who are not baptized. They contend that given that given the fact that the nation – state is a composition of people from different cultures and tribes, atheists and believers, it is the nation-state that is Catholic and not the Church (see Cavanaugh 2011:1-5). Such an assumption misses a point. In fact theologically, these people miss a big point. They look at the Church just like a social institution. They forget its universal dimension and non exclusive nature. They overlook the fact that the Church is a mystery and according to St. Augustine it has existed from the time of Abel. Theologically they undermine the first statement of the Dogmatic Constitution that "Christ is the light of the Nations." The Church is in the world not only for those within her by baptism, but all the human family. In this sense, one can justly state that Christology has precedence over ecclesiology. Thus, 'the church was Catholic even in the catacombs. Salvation history is not a subject of world history, but simply is the history – not yet complete or legible of human action in a grace – soaked world' (Cavanaugh 2011:1-5).

To say that the community of faith, the Church has a political witness does not mean to reject the separation of Church and State. The Church is striving to make known the values of the kingdom. However, 'the pursuit of justice must be fundamental norm of the state and that the aim of just social order is to guarantee to each person, according to the principle of subsidiary, his share of the community's good' (Benedict XVI 2005: no. 26).

There is a good reason to limit ecclesiastical authorities from wielding power on secular matters. The Church is not *polis* but an *ekklesia*. This is not as equal as to restrict the Church exclusively in spiritual matters. As a pilgrim community, as a little flock of the Lord, the Church is not in the world to dominate castles and palaces of the ruling class, but to witness love in truth. She has a mission to preach God's design for the world. To ensure that the common good is upheld for all, and the human fraternity is steadily constructed and the solidarity of nations prospers, the Church need to cooperate with nation – states.

The Vatican State: Chair of Charity and Truth

Rome is the chair of Christian charity. The Holy See is not simply an administration compound, but it is where the Christians are rallied to be of one heart with fellow human beings worldwide. The Holy Father through the generous contributions from generous Catholic faithful is deeply engaged in assisting those in need.

The Catholic Church is one of the most visible solidarity synergy across the globe. From Rome to all dioceses in the world, there exists a creative networking of caritas. Through Church agencies the Church takes part in alleviating the plights of the people in need. Generosity and hospitality are characteristics of faith community. The Holy Father himself promotes the corporal works of mercy. He mobilizes the *Peters' pence* which is the financial support arm of the Bishop of Rome. It is sustained by generous contribution which is made by the Catholic faithful worldwide.

There is also the Pontifical Council *Cor unum* which works for Human and Christian Development. It is part of the curia of the Catholic Church. It is in existence since 1971, created by Pope Paul VI to manifest the heart of Christ, who opted to be in solidarity with the hungry multitudes by reaching them and feeding them. This Pontifical Council encourages human fellowship and the making manifest the charity of Christ. Other institutions worth to mention are the *Caritas Internationalis* and *Missio* (Aachen and München) which help to strengthen the care of the Holy Father for young churches and communities in global South.

Besides having organizations that promote charity and compassion for the needy, the Vatican State pursues the common good together with other global players. It takes part in international meetings organized by the United Nations, European Union, and the African Union, etc. This helps the Vatican to follow closely contemporary issues which face the world like migrations, nuclear threats, environmental disasters, pollution and other issues. Such awareness helps the Roman Catholic Church to address contemporary issues with effective pastoral strategies.

Through its representative in international meeting, the Holy See has influenced major decisions for the protection of human dignity and justice. It is significant to mention the United Nations Conference on Women held in Beijing China in 1994. The United States at the time was under the presidency of Bill Clinton. The country was determined to push forward the agenda to legalize abortion and family planning more accessible to women in the Majority World, reasoning that in those poor countries, the women bear a scar of societal burdens of child rearing. The Vatican and representatives of Muslim countries worked hard to block the Us-led campaign in favour of abortion law (see Manuel 2008:204). The Holy See has signed on to a number of international agreements such as the International Convention on the Elimination of All Forms of Racial Discrimination. The International Convention on Rights of the Child, a treaty on the Non-Proliferation of Nuclear Weapons, the Convention of UNESCO for the Protection of World Cultural and Nature, and many of such conventions which are destined to safeguard human life and dignity and that of the creation as a whole.

Fostering Dialogue with Human Family

The second advantage is in the area of dialogue. The Vatican State has organized conferences and workshops to discuss about peace and reconciliation and other issues. The position of the Vatican has been made known at the international platform. With competent diplomatic service, such as that managed by the late Secretary of State

Cardinal Agostino Cassarolli (24 November 1914 - 9 June 1998), the Vatican engineered a fruitful dialogue with both the Russian government and the Orthodox Church for the acceptance of the Roman Catholic Church in Russia. Cassaroli also played a significant diplomatic role in Eastern Europe, for the peaceful transition from communism to liberalism. 'At the global level, the Vatican has been especially supportive of the role of the United Nations and transnational organizations' (Hanson 2011:214). The high point of Cardinal Casaroli's diplomatic career came in 1989, a year before his retirement, when he helped arrange the historic meeting between the Soviet leader Mikhail Gorbachev and Pope John Paul II at the Vatican. After the death of the Cardinal, Pope John Paul described him "as impassioned weaver of peaceful relations between individuals and nations, carrying out courageous and meaningful steps with fine diplomatic sensitivity...in particular to improve the situation of the Church in Eastern Europe." And because of his diplomatic skills, in his efforts to restore diplomatic ties with the Soviet bloc, the cardinal was regarded in diplomatic circles as "the Pope's Henry Kissinger." Kissinger was a renowned U.S Secretary of State during the time of President Richard Nixon.

Relations with Nation - States

As an independent State, the Vatican has diplomatic relations with different countries. The Apostolic Nuncios are representatives of the Pope in the countries they are accredited. This incorporates the Vatican State in the Diplomatic network of nation states.

Recently there has been an increasing voice from the South on the unfair display of diplomatic relation at work. The poor nations feel that the diplomatic plain is dominated by nations entitled with VETO deliberative votes; the five permanent members of the Security Countries including the United States, United Kingdom, Germany, France, China, and Russia. The African continent with 54 countries including Southern Sudan has no representative, let alone the Latin American continent. Moreover, some analysts complain that some Western ambassadors do not respect the priorities of the nation states (see *NewAfrican* July 2011:9). The Western embassies resort to lecturing and putting pressures on African governments. Ambassadors from the industrialized world use press conferences, non-government organisations and non-governmental individuals to pressurize African countries to do things which in some cases are not the priority of the people. The developing countries are tamed by donors' money they need to enable national budget work. At the diplomatic scene it is a common thing to see Western ambassadors in Africa openly criticizing the African governments, something which runs contrary to diplomatic relations. Indeed the African ambassadors do not call press conferences in London, Washington, and Paris for example to express their criticism against Western policies. This is not to say that they do not have their grievances. Simply, there is a fear to destroying diplomatic harmony and eventually suspension of aids. The diplomatic corps of the Holy See may not be involved in this kind of "lecturing," but since the Apostolic Nuncio plays the role as Dean of the Foreign Ambassadors, diplomatic tensions indirectly involves them as well.

In the world with many conflicts, diplomatic relations faces a hard task. The Pope as head of state is bound also to diplomatic ethics and has to be careful not to pronounce words that may complicate the relationship between nation states. As globally high respected person he is compelled to defend the truth.

The recent popes have been critical to both capitalism and socialism. This is because, 'the popes have feared three troubling characteristics of the growing socialist movement: its emphasis on materialism, its willingness to use violence to achieve its objectives, and its hostility toward religion' (Manuel 2008:206). On the other hand Vatican is also critical of the American capitalistic ambitions, 'the Vatican worldviews represents something of a challenge for American economic policies. The century-long tradition of Catholic Social Teaching challenges the citizens to think in terms of community, with preference for the poor and vulnerable in society' (Manuel 2008:207).

In serving the will of God rather than that of the human persons, the Pope will always be in conflict with nation states. We take the example of China. The Vatican State has no diplomatic relationship with China so far. There are some issues to settle. The government in China supports the National Catholic Church of which it has influence in the appointment of bishops. This is against the canonical regulation on how bishops in the Roman Catholic Church are appointed. It is the pejorative of the Holy Father to name new bishops. The policy of the Roman Catholic Church and that of the nation – state in China may not get together easily. The Church for this matter justly supports the separation of religion and politics. This helps to promote the separation of one's loyalty to the church from one's loyalty to nation state, and thus the "migration of the holy" (Bossy 1985:153-71).

With situation like this one above, the Pope as head of state faces some daunting challenging situations as whether to remain on a diplomatic plane to issues which as spiritual leader should not. Is the Pope to keep silent not to challenge Hamas or the Hezbollah, when they attack some targets in Israel for fear that he is going to irritate the Muslim world? Should the Pope pronounce diplomatic statements to Israel, if its soldiers do not show restraint when some Hamas militias target innocent people in the Jewish State? Bound by diplomatic discretion as head of State; should the Pope keep quite in such circumstances so that not to harm the relationship with nation states? St. Paul admonishes Timothy, "proclaim the message; be persistent whether the time is favourable or unfavourable; convince, rebuke, and encourage, with utmost patience in teaching...As for you, always be sober, endure suffering, do the work of an evangelist, carry out your ministry fully" (2 Tim 4:3-5).

Demanding the Pope to keep neutrality in every situation of conflict, and therefore not to show partiality, will be a mistake. The first mistake takes 'the assumption that all conflicts are based upon misunderstanding and that blame always exists on both sides...The assumption is unfounded and has nothing whatsoever to do with Christianity. This assumption could only be made by people who do not suffer under injustice and oppression or who do not really appreciate the sinfulness and evil of what is happening' (Nolan 2008:65). To think that the Holy Father as religious leader should be always neutral as has been upheld over all these years is a mistake, because 'it assumes that a person can be neutral in all cases of conflict. In fact, neutrality is not always possible, and in cases of conflict due to injustice and oppression, neutrality is totally impossible. If we do not take sides with the oppressed, then we are albeit unintentionally, taking sides with the oppressor' (Nolan 2008:65). Then we come to the last mistake in which many people want the Pope and the Church to always seek harmony and a middle way in every friction between conflicting parties. 'This false supposition is again based upon a lack of compassion for those who suffer under oppression. People who are afraid of conflict or confrontation, even when it is non violent, are always those who are not convinced of the need for change. Their caution hides an unchristian pessimism about the future, a lack of hope' (Nolan 2008:66). Given the contemporary situation, the Pope must speak out and teach the will of Christ. In doing that he is going to irritate governments and risk his security. It is important for the Catholic faithful to know of the duty to protect the Pope in his struggle to defend justice in the world.

All in all, the position of the Pope as head of state cannot avoid tensions. Any kind of human relation involves moments of harmony and tensions as well. The Church made up of human being prone with weakness is not spared in making decisions which may become controversial. This may happen in making political statements and even in some ecclesiastical teachings and decisions. A concrete example can be taken from the debate which ensued after the University of Notre Dame had honoured President Barack Obama to make a 2009 commencement address. The administration of the University got into trouble with U.S Catholic bishops about the decision to invite President Obama there. Those who differed with the position of the bishops wondered as to what was wrong for an academic institution like the Notre Dame not to accord the President such honour. They doubted as to whether the bishops had no hidden political agenda. This they believed because some days before Pope Benedict XVI himself made former French Nicolas Sarkozy an honorary canon of St. John Lateran's. 'And he (President Nicolas Sarkozy) is pro-abortion, pro-gay marriage married invalidly to an actress, and the Pope did that' (Roberts 2011:156).

In diplomatic relations between the Church and the nation states is not a different case. The Holy See has been in diplomatic relations with different nations under their different forms of governments, at times including dictatorial regimes as well. This being the case however, at times the Church has not been prophetic and critical enough to the authoritarian regimes. Yet, at times she has cooperated with dictatorial regime. In the context of rebellion in which we live today, there is need for the Church to take a bold stance about her diplomatic relationship with dictatorial regimes. Let us now look at some of the examples:

Military Junta in Brazil
The Blessed Pope John Paul II made his first visit in Brazil, when the country was under military rule. The country has as from 31 March, 1964 to March 15, 1985 been ruled by the military junta. This regime has been abusing human rights and oppressing workers by paying them low wages. The then Archbishop of Sao Paulo, cardinal Paulo Evaristo Arns was a staunch defender of human right. His uncompromising advocacy for the poor won him the heart of many people. The cardinal was involved in human rights struggle. Some few months before the Pope John Paul II visited Brazil, the military's secret police raided a priest's house where they found papers advocating better wages for workers. Using these papers as alleged proof of "subversiveness," the police brutally tortured the priest and his assistant. When cardinal Arns learned of the arrest, he went to the governor's office to protest and then to the prison where he was denied entrance. Outraged, he denounced the incident in the archdiocese's newspaper and its radio station. He ordered the

description of the arrest to be nailed to the door of every church in the city.

The relationship between the military junta and the Brazilian Church was not good. When Pope John Paul II arrived in Brazil, the Junta had organized a military chopper (helicopter) to transport the Pope to a remote part of Brazil where he celebrated a Pontifical Mass. The Brazilian Episcopal Conference had also organized its own modest means of transporting him to the same venue. The Holy Father had to decide either to use the means provided by the State which had arranged through the Papal nuncio to provide the Pope with a "more secure means of transport" or take risk of using a "fragile transport" provided by the bishops. Cardinal Paulo Evaristo Arns cautioned the Pope to be careful for if he travels with the state he opts to be with the military, but if he takes the transport arranged by the Church in Brazil, he takes side with the people (see Allen 2000:114ff). The Holy Father opted to travel with the Church.

General Augusto Pinochet's Saga

There is another incident to be mentioned here. It is related to the controversy which surrounded the Chilean dictator. This episode followed the arrest of the late General Augusto Pinochet in London in October 1998. The arrest was made at the request of Spain. The former Chile colonial master, who petitioned that the dictator be extradited to Spain to stand trial for mass killings and torture of his own people while in power, Pope John Paul II made an appeal to the British government for the release of Augusto Pinochet "for humanitarian reasons." This appeal by the head of Vatican State outraged human rights groups and relatives of the victims of Pinochet's murderous regime in Chile. Some sources report that the General had good relationship with Angelo Sodano who was papal Nuncio in Chile during Pinochet's reign, and maintained a close friendship. The Cardinal was later promoted by Pope John Paul II to become the Secretary of the State after the retirement of Cardinal Agostino Casarolli. Augusto Pinochet, some claim, won the support of the Vatican at the time for the credentials of his Catholic faith and his campaign against Marxism, which was compatible with the struggles of Pope John Paul II against communism.

The Pope and the Holy See made clear that it appealed for General Pinochet's release for, humanitarian reasons with the aim to facilitate the process of reconciliation amongst Chileans. There were groups of people who chose to differ with the official position of the Holy See. The groups included theologians, human right activists, and lawyers. For these groups, the Pope's humanitarian concern for a man who directed the extermination and torture of tens of thousands of workers, students and intellectuals was incomprehensible.

The Manuel Noriega Drama

Another incident is that which took place at the Vatican embassy in Panama. General Manuel Antonio Noriega had been assisted by Americans to come to power in 1983. During his reign however, he supported the drug cartel and was implicated in trafficking Marijuana and drugs. He also ordered the killings of his opponents. When the American discovered that General Noriega was pursuing socialist policies, taking sides with Cuba, they decided to oust him. The Pentagon organized the Operation Nifty Package which involved about 48 Navy SEALs- with the mandate to capture Noriega and bring him to America to face charges. During the operation, Manuel Noriega fled the attack and the manhunt ensued. After threatening that he would call for guerrilla warfare if the Apostolic Nuncio did not give him refuge, he was found to have taken refuge in the Apostolic Nunciature in Panama. The American soldiers surrounded the Vatican Embassy, and deliberately distracted the Archbishop and his staff with loud, thematic rock music (such as "smugglers Blues," "Nowhere to Run," and "Voodoo Chile"). It was a psychological warfare which was supported by a continuous noise from a low flying helicopter. 'While the White house characterized this technological and psychological warfare as "fairly standard practice," the Vatican portrayed the actions as "ludicrous" and "childish" violations of international law and diplomatic norms'(Carty 2008:188). Let it be known to the reader that, the Vatican embassy did not have friendly relationship with Manuel Noriega. The Nuncio did not invite the General, rather the General forced his way threatening that if the Nuntiature did not accommodate him he is going to resort into bloodshed by starting guerrilla warfare. The Nuncio in Panama accepted him temporarily to avoid the possibility of bloodshed.

In relationship with nation states the Church cannot avoid conflicts with some of them. Conflicts may happen now and then given the complicated landscape of unjust relationship between the nations. In her relations with nation – states the Church must face conflicts and consider them as chance to promote dialogue. According to William Cavanaugh, 'the church, must be hospitable to conflict if it is to remain penitent and therefore faithful to Christ. Those who want to follow the way of Christ must always recognize that Christ is in an exile from their own communities' (Cavanaugh 2011:193).

Concluding Reflections

Issues of human security, human rights and dignity have of late emerged as crucial references in Church's social teachings and in the work of some theologians. For this matter we have discovered the urgency of the theme of security for the Holy Father and all members of the Church. In treating the theme, we have repeatedly underlined the concepts of *security* and *protection*. These two words are not identical. The word "security" is used to indicate an absence of violence to the physical body, "protection" on its part entails all what is necessary for the creation of security. It is with this understanding that the social documents of the Church strongly calls for the protection of the life of every human person including the unborn child. Therefore, a treatise about security cannot be regarded as an extra-ecclesia topic. It has pastoral and moral imperatives in ecclesiastical disciplines in so far as human rights and human justice are concerned.

The Christian faithful all over the world face danger for their lives and dignity. News of churches being burnt down is on increase. Christians are targeted in house of prayers. Not few of them are killed. Death is on their sight. This book appeals for increased vigilance against such backdrops. This does not mean that we want to plead to Christians to take a negative view about death. A Christian is admonished not to worry about death but to anticipate it with hope and courage. The old adage goes *memento mori* meaning "remember death." This adage is not intended to condemn us to resignation of perpetual fear in face of death. It is neither to be seen as a negative admonition, nor as a discouragement but as a reminder to stay awake. We should be awake against the forgetfulness of what we are and what we are destined to be. To appreciate better the liberty of the children of God, we have to embrace the spirit of dispossession. We must live the "dying in order to live" by freeing ourselves from the chains of materialism. St. Francis of Assisi distanced himself from material security and as a result was befriended with death. Thus he could describe not without reason, that death was a brother to him, "Ooh Brother Death."

During the sacrament of baptism, a newly baptized is not only reminded of his/her death but also of the resurrection. At the baptismal font the waters are poured on his/her body with the baptismal formula. It is a passage from death to life. Then, the newly born in faith is clothed with new garments and is told to hold the burning candle as sign of the risen Lord. The Easter event is linked to the Pentecostal event as one event. In that sense, the sacrament of baptism and confirmation are closely tied together. A Christian is confirmed by the power or the Holy Spirit to endure tribulations and persecutions. In the past the Bishop who ministered the sacrament of confirmation concluded the administering of confirmation by slapping the cheek of the newly confirmed to admonish him or her to live the faith with courage. In this way the Christians lived with the knowledge that any given moment they could be subjected to pay the price for their being baptized. The early Christians for example, developed an understanding of two types of baptism: the first one by water in the Church and the second one by blood in the arena. To be baptized in the early centuries of Christianity provided one with an apparent danger of being assassinated. From its very infant stage, Christianity trained the faithful to regard themselves to be alien to the standards of worldly powers.

The threat for life against those who preach justice, the love of the neighbour and truth of the Word of God is a reality of today. The Christian faithful are called to confront the injustice of this world. Part of their mission is to face those on power, who will always cry out with loud voice as the people of Thessalonica did when Paul and Silas visited their city: "those who turn everything upside down are here. They are out to destroy the world and now they are here on our door steps, attacking everything we hold dear" (Act 17:6). They will not abandon power, profit, position, or possession. If due to fear of consequences, we hold our tongue and don't offer critics, we shake the integrity of our discipleship.

At every time of Church history a Christian faithful has to show a committed zeal to discipleship. The witness of the faith became a *conditio sine quo non* for the early Christians, as it is for Christians of today. The early Christians confronted the persecutions with a bold stance of martyrdom. Some of them had to shed their blood. When the persecution period ended, Christianity was declared a "State Religion." Now it was accorded its security and other privileges by the power of the Empire. The Church embraced a "secular security." Some Christian faithful at the time observed that something was at stake, and therefore a new kind of witness had to be invented. Personalities like St. Antonius, St. Pachomius, St. Benedict and many others founded a new life of poverty, prayer and contemplation, thus paving way for the beginning of monasticism. The monasteries for men and convents for women developed themselves as protest to secular and worldly elements of power which had entered the Church. What emerged from this form of witness was simplicity in lifestyle, lateral relationship between confreres, and the life of service. As monasteries opened schools and hospitals which cared for the sick, the witness was centred on *diakonia* and *caritas*.

In the violent and aggressive world we live today, Christians have to invent new forms of witness. 'A divided world needs people with vision, spiritual maturity and daily skills integral to the journey of reconciliation' (Hauerwas: Vanier 2008:8). There is an urgent need for a witness to non violence. The practices of non violence call for a changed heart. It presupposes a completely new way of positioning ourselves in relation to power. 'Non violence is a way of ordering our lives so that everyone will be empowered; it refers to people who discipline themselves to be gentle rather than severe' (Crosby 2008:141). The sermon on the mountains pronounces blessedness to peace makers, it states 'Blessed are the peace makers, for they will be called children of God' (Mt 5:9). Christians must renounce violence. In "Everything Depends on Your Peace," the Buddhist monk Thich Nhat Hans writes: '...our strength is not in weapons, money, or power. Our strength is in our peace, the peace within us' (Crosby 2008:150). The paradox however is that, the more we try to become peacemakers, the more we become ourselves the target of the very violence we turn against. The evil forces however, do not have the last word. The Christian believer is not to be blinded with worldly security. 'Church resistance to violence should not be based on the view of the church as a perfect society, but rather on the penitential recognition that we are incapable of using violence justly' (Cavanaugh 2011:4).

The security of the Pope and other members of the Church remain under severe test. The new direction the Church is taking for its commitment to the cause of human rights and justice means that she is going to be in constant conflicts with those who oppress and discriminate against the poor. ' Christians are at work in a world they do not own, but within which they have a calling to serve God's purpose-not to turn the world into more property and power for churches, but encourage human flourishing within all religions, all institutions, all nations, each in its own way' (Johnson 2007:165). Even at this time of insecurity the occupation of the Church should not be to build walls and close itself up. 'The challenge for the Church is to become the sort of community that can speak convincingly about God, which is to say a place of mercy and mutual delight, of joy and freedom' (Raddclife 2005:210).

Christians are surrounded with world stories and media coverage which precipitate fear and worries. We are human beings just like others. As people who are bonded by faith, love and hope, however, we are connected with a light even in the midst of darkest night. We are guided by the Holy Spirit who help us to recognize the contrasting aspects of night. We must understand that the dawn emerges after passing the experience of the darkest night. We have to dive courageously to overcome the fear-engendering darkness. The Pope and all Christian faithful are plunged into the darkness of Good Friday, but lifted up by the power of the risen Lord. We are at the same time consoled with the breezes of the Easter dawn. Thus we can endure successfully the tension between, "fear not" for those who kill the body and cannot kill the soul, and "for they were afraid," at the awe of the divine presence who does not abandon us.

In order to live in harmony and peace we have to follow the road of dispossession. A Christian conduct should be marked by simplicity in living which does not count on palaces, financial power, and worldly glory as security fortress. Rather, the human security begins with the fear of the Lord, *timor Domini*. Perhaps the critical challenge facing the Pope on top down to the ordinary Christian faithful at grassroots today; is how to become witnesses of peace in the current wave of violence. We live in a situation which we may find ourselves called to revenge and make a reasonable retaliation by pursuing violence. Such circumstances may prove difficult to grasp the wisdom of the one Crucified. It is important to listen to the wise words of Archbishop Oscar Romeo "a Church that does not suffer persecution should fear for itself. It is not the true Church of Jesus Christ" (Sobrino 2008:94).

The Christian faithful hold that Jesus Christ whom they follow is the Prince of Peace. Jesus the Christ is referred also as the *Lion of Juda* (see Rev. 5:5). The image of a Lion represents strength and majesty; where as that of the Lamb puts forward the qualities such as gentleness, kindness and caring. In the midst of persecution the Christian faithful can endure all these tribulations, for he/she is sure that Jesus Christ is also the "Lion of Juda." Jesus Christ the Lord has ability to execute judgement. Theologian Miroslav Volf makes a point: 'without entrusting oneself to the God who judges justly, it will hardly be possible to follow the crucified Messiah and refuse to retaliate when abused. The certainty of God's just judgment at the end of history; is the presupposition for the renunciation of violence in the middle of it' (Volf 1996: 302). The early Christians were alive with the knowledge of eschatological advent of Christ as Judge of the Universe. They endured the persecutions with steadfast courage. Tertullian qualified the Christians as those destined to be innocent preys to lions *"Christianos ad leones."* This is truly so given the situation which Christians in the primitive Church had confronted as it is for Christians living today. In the world where nation states are obsessed with power and material prosperity, which often time facilitate unjust competitions and unjust wars, churches are outspoken. The more they criticize the injustices committed, the more church personnel are targeted as enemies. To speak the truth and oppose to violence requires humility. In a situation of sufferings, let us be motivated by the boldness of our ancestors in faith: the martyrs, whose memory from the catacombs and the coliseum keep our minds alive; this is a cause of much hope for the Christians of today.

There is a tension between life and death as the *Exsultet* speaks, the song which is solemnly sung at Easter vigil. The Christians celebrate death but also proclaim it as a passage to life. The interpretation of death by Pilate, Herod and the Roman authorities differs very much with the manner to which Jesus and the early Christians saw it. For Jesus, Stephan and many other martyrs, death became an ongoing process towards glorification. It was a surrendering love, and an expression of that love. That is why the first time the concept "love" appears in the Bible is at the time when Abraham is ordered by God to sacrifice his only son Isaac. "Take your son, your only son Isaac, whom you love" (Gen 22:2). For imperial Rome death of the Christians was inflicted because of hate and the passion to preserve power. Pilate who represents the imperial hegemony seals the tomb where Jesus Christ is buried and with this seal he is determined to terminate all subversive attempts against the empire.

To this point one understands now that the proposal made by the journalist in the *ABC Australia* column as quoted at the introduction of this book, notably to bomb the Vatican and to hunt for the Pope in order to eliminate him is not a mere fiction, it is a spark of the violent world that we live in. And that the question Peter Seewald asked the Pope "Are you afraid of an assassination attempt?" is a result of careful reading of the signs of time. Consequently, the reply "No" of the Pope is a manifestation of a courageous Christian. It should be taken as a compass for the persecuted Christian minority in secularized world of today. The answer "No" wants to remind Christians to have no fear. Reading the Bible, the formulation "do not have fear" appears 366 times. This means that within a year which has about 365 days, a Christian faithful is assured by God everyday "have no fear, I am with you." The settling words "do not have fear" as they are traced in the Bible, are addressed to human beings in different situation. One finds it at a moment when human life is threatened by natural catastrophes such as the stormy waters in the sea. They are also addressed at the time when human life is threatened by human inclination to violence. Yet, in some cases they are spoken at a time when human life is clinically and mechanically terminated, where death is recognized and necrology spread. The bringing back to life by Jesus Christ of personalities whose death are publicly acknowledged such as the daughter of Jairus, the young man at Naim and Lazarus at Bethany justifies the proposition "have no fear at all." After his resurrection, the Lord strongly reassures the apostles, "to have no fear." The risen Christ thwarts all attempts of state's apparatus to crown death. The empty tomb breaks the seal of the secular empire and paralyzes the morale of the soldiers to continue guarding the tomb. The risen Lord cannot be hindered by a momentum of secular rage. Therefore, to close the chapters of this book it is noteworthy to borrow the words of the Blessed John Paul II: "Christ our Hope is alive; we shall live!" (John Paul II 1995, no. 13)

Selected Bibliography

Alexseev, Mikhail. A., "Societal security, the security dilemma, and extreme anti-migrants hostility in Russia" in *Journal of Peace Research* 48 (2011), 509-523

Allen, John. L. JR., *Cardinal Ratzinger: Vatican's Enforcer of the Faith*, London: Continuum, 2000

-------------------------., *The Future Church: How Ten Trends Are Revolutionizing the Catholic Church*, New York: Doubleday, 2009

Alvarez, David., *The Pope's Soldiers: A Military History of the Modern Vatican*, Kansas: The University of Kansas Press, 2011

Araujo, Robert John and John A. Lucal., *Papal Diplomacy and the Quest for Peace – The United Nations from Pius XII to Paul VI*, Philadelphia: Saint Joseph University Press, 2010

Barron, Robert., *Catholicism: A Journey to the Heart of the Faith*, New York: Image Books, 2011

Baum, Gregory., *Amazing Church: A Catholic Theologian Remembers a Half-Century of Change*, Maryknoll, N.Y: Orbis Books, 2005

BBC News., "Obama in the UK: The Security Cordon" (24 May 2011) in http://www.bbc.co.uk/news/world-us-canada 13475162 (accessed on 30 August 2011)

Becker-Huberti, Manfred., *Feiern, Feste, Jahreszeiten*, Freiburg im Breisgau: Herder, 2001

Becker, William. M., "The Flag of Vatican City" 2008 in http://vatflag.tripod.com (accessed on 12.07.2011)

Benedict XVI., *Let God's Light Shine Forth* (Robert Moyniham, editor), New York: Doubleday, 2005

----------------------Encyclical Letter *Deus Caritas Est*, Vatican City, 2005

---------------------., *Light of the World: The Pope, the Church, and the Signs of the Time* (conversation with Peter Seewald), Nairobi: Paulines Publications Africa, 2010

----------------------., "Religious Freedom, the Path to Peace" *Message of His Holiness Pope Benedict XVI for the Celebration of the World Day of Peace*, (1 January 2011) in http://www.vatican.va/holy_father/benedict_xvi/messages/peace/documents/hf_ben-xvi_mes-20101208_xliv-world-day-peace-en.html (accessed on 26/01/2012)

Body, Brady., *Fear no Evil: A Test of Faith, a Courageous Church, and an Unfailing God*, Grand Rapids, MI: Zondervan, 2011

Bossy, John., *Christianity in the West, 1400-1700*, Oxford: Oxford University Press, 1985

Bouma-Prediger, Steven and Walsch, Brian. J., *Beyond Homelessness: Christian Faith in a Culture of Displacement*, Grand Rapids, Michigan: Eerdmans Publishing, 2008

Brown, Raymond., *Death of the Messiah*, Vol. 1 New York: Doubleday, 1994

Brueggemann, Walter., *Truth – Telling as Subversive Obedience*, Eugene, Oregon: Cascade Books, 2011

Budde, Michael. L and Scott, Karen (eds.)., *Witness of the Body: The Past, Present, and Future of the Christian Martyrdom*, Grand Rapids, Michigan: Eerdmans Publishing, 2011

Budde, Michael. L., *The Borders of Baptism: Identities, Allegiances, and the Church*, Eugence, Oregon: CASCADE Books, 2011

Camp, Lee. C., *Mere Discipleship: Radical Christianity in a Rebellious World*, Grand Rapids, Michigan: Brazos Press, 2008

Cantalamesa, Raniero., *Sober Intoxication of the Spirit: Filled with the Spirit of God*, Cincinnati: Servant Books, 2005

Carry, Thomas, S.J., "White House Outreach to Catholics" in Kristin E. Heyer et al. (eds.)., *Catholics and Politics: The Dynamic Tension Between Faith and Power*, Washington, DC: Georgetown University Press, 2008

Cavanaugh, William. T., *Migrations of the Holy: God, State, and the Political Meaning of the Church*, Grand Rapids, Michigan: Eerdmans Publishing, 2011

----------------------------., "Destroying the Church to Save It: Intra-Christian Persecution and the Modern State" in Budde, Michael,

L and Karen Scott., *Witness of the Body: The Past, Present, and Future of Christian Martyrdom*, Grand Rapids, Michigan: Eerdmans Publishing, 2011

Collins, Michael., "Comments on 'The Vatican as a State'" in http://www.slaw.ca/2010/09/14/the-vatican-as-a-state (accessed 12.08.2011)

Coren, Michael., *Why Catholics are Right*, Toronto: McClelland & Steward Ltd, 2012

Crosby, Michael. H., *The Paradox of Power: From Control to Compassion*, New York: Crossroad, 2008

Cunningham, Lawrence., "Christian Martyrdom: A Theological Perspective" in Michael L. Budde and Karen Scott (eds.)., *Witness of the Body: The Past, Present, and Future of Christian Martyrdom*, Grand Rapids, Michigan: Eerdmans Publishing, 2011

DECOSSE, David, E., "Authority, Lies, and War: Democracy and the Development of Just War Theory" in *Theological Studies* 67 (2006)

Englisch, Andreas., *Johannes Paul II: Das Geheimnis des Karol Wojtyla*, München: Ullstein, 2003

Erskine, Toni., "Kicking Bodies and Damning Souls: The Danger of Harming 'Innocent' Individuals while punishing 'Delinquent States'" in *Ethics and International Affairs*, vol. 24 (2010)

Fodden, Simon., "The Vatican as a State" in http://www.slaw.ca/2010/09/14/the-vatican-as-a-state (accessed 12.08.2011)

Forte, David. F., "A Sign of Contradiction" in *University of St. Thomas Journal of Law and Public Policy*, Vol. 1.1 (2007)

Garrity Ranaghan, Dorothy., *Blind Spot: War and Christian Identity*, Hyde Park, N.Y: New City Press, 2011

Goliama, Castor. M., *Where Are you Africa: Church and Society in Mobile Phone Age*, Bamenda: Langaa Publishers, 2011

Grayson, Kyle., "The Ambivalence of Assassination: Bio-politics, Culture and Political Violence" in *Security Dialogue* 43 (2012)

Hanson, Erick. O., "Flashpoints for Future Martyrdom: Beyond the "Clash of Civilizations" in Michael L. Budde and Karen Scott (eds.)., *Witness of the Body: The Past, Present, and Future of Christian Martyrdom*, Grand Rapids, Michigan: Eerdmans Publishing, 2011

Harrington, Wilfrid. J, OP., *Jesus our Brother: The Humanity of the Lord*, New York/Mahwah, NJ: Paulist Press, 2010

Hauerwas, Stanley and Vanier, Jean., *Living Gently in a Violent World: The Prophetic Witness of Weakness*, Downers Grove, Illonois: IVP Books, 2008

Huntington, Samuel., *The Clash of Civilization and the Remaking of the World Order*, New York: Touchstone, 1996

Jenkins, Philip., *God's Continent: Christianity, Islam, and Europe's Religious Crisis*, Oxford: Oxford University Press, 2007

John Paul II, Apostolic Exhortation, *Ecclesia in Africa*, Vatican City, 1995

Juergensmeyer, Mark., *Global Rebellion: Religious Challenges to the Secular State, from Christian Militias to Al Qaeda*, Berkeley: University of California Press, 2008

Katongole, Emmanuel., *A Future for Africa: Critical Essays in Christian Social Imagination*, Scranton: The University of Scranton Press, 2005

Kelsay, John., "Just War, Jihad, and the Study of Comparative Ethics" in *Ethics and International Affairs*, vol. 24 (2010)

Kerr, David., "Vatican's Idea for Day against Christian Persecution draws Praise" *Catholicnewsagency* in http://www.catholicnewsagency.com/news/vaticans-idea-for-day-against-christian-per (accessed 26/01/2012)

Kim, Nami., "A Mission to the "Graveyard of Empires"? Neocolonialism and the Contemporary Evangelical Mission of the Global South" in *Mission Studies* 27 (2010)

Lash, Nicholas., *Theology for Pilgrims*, Notre Dame, Indiana: University of Notre Dame Press, 2008

Ledewitz, Bruce., *Church, State, and the Crisis of American Secularism*, Notre Dame, Indiana: University of Indiana Press, 2011

Leyton, Richards., "Christian Pacifism After Two World Wars" quoted in *Provocative Pamphlets* (July 1957) in http://www.mun.ca/rels/restmov/texts/pp/pp031.HTM (accessed 12 December 2011)

MacPherson, D. Neal. *The Church at a Crossroads: Being the Church after Christendom*: Eugene: Wipf and Stock, 2008

Mannion, Gerard., *Ecclesiology and Post Modernity: Questions for the Church in our Time*, Collegeville, Minnesota: Liturgical Press, 2007

McCarthy, "Quo Vadis" in The Catholic University of America, *New Catholic Encyclopaedia* (Second Edition), Washington Dc: The Catholic University of America, 2003

Miehle, Wolfgan., "Charity and Service to Users of the Road and Railway" in *People on the Move*, December, 2010

Nolan, Albert., *Jesus Today: A Spirituality of Radical Freedom*, Maryknoll, N.Y: Orbis Books, 2006

--------------------., *Hope in an Age of Despair*, Maryknoll, N.Y: Orbis Books, 2009

North Carolina Department of Correction., "Assigning Inmates to Prison" in http;//www.doc.state.nc.us/dop/custody.htm (accessed on 12.07.2011)

Nyenyembe, Jordan., *Papa Benedikto XVI (Joseph Ratzinger): Upapa katika Mwelekeo Upi?* Dar-es-Salaam: Eco Print, 2005

----------------------., *Spirituality in African Sports: Version of Public Religion*, Sassenbrucker: Dr. Müller Verlag, 2010

O'Connell, Maureen. H., *Compassion: Loving Our Neighbor in an Age of Globalization*, Maryknoll, N.Y: Orbis Books, 2009

O' Murch, Diarmuid., *Ancestral Grace: Meeting God in Our Human Story*, Maryknoll, N.Y: Orbis Books, 2008

Ott, Craig and Netland, Harold A., *Globalizing Theology*, Grand Rapids, Michigan: Baker Academic, 2008

Paul VI., "Statement on Disarmament" Vatican City, 1975 in http://www.vatican.va/holy_father/paul_vi/messages/peace/documents/hf_p-vi_mes_19751018_ix-world-day-for-peace_en.html (accessed 12 August 2011)

Perabo, Betsy., "How Soldiers Too, Can Be Saved: Allegiance and Idolatry in the US Military" in *Political Theology* (2010), 247-270

Porter, Bruce D., *War and the Rise of the State: The Military Foundations of Modern Politics*, New York: Free Press, 1994

Riggio, Andres., "The Catholic Church is Dangerous, Outdated, and should Dissolve" in http://news.yahoo.com/Catholic.Church-dangerous-outdated-dissolve-204000761.h (accessed 3 June 2012)

Roberts, Tom., *The Emerging Catholic Church: A Community's Search for Itself*, Maryknoll, N.Y: Orbis Books, 2011

Royal, Robert, *The Pope's Army: 500 Years of the Papal Swiss Guard*, New York: The Crossroad Publishing Company, 2006

Ryan, Cheyney., "Democratic Duty and the Moral Dilemmas of Soldiers" in *Ethics* 122 (October 2011), 10-42

Ratzinger, Cardinal Joseph., *Values in a Time of Upheaval*, New York: Crossroads, Ignatius, 2006

Sandler, Todd., "New Frontiers of Terrorism Research: An Introduction" in *Journal of Peace Research* 48 (2011), 297-286

Schanbacher, William. D., *The Politics of Food*, Sancta Barbara, California: Praeger, 2010

Sheppard, Grace., *An Aspect of Fear: A Journey from Anxiety to Peace*, London: Darton. Longman+Todd, 2011 (Edition)

Schönbonn, Cardinal Christoph.,"Johannes Paul der Große: Ein Fels des Gebetes, ein Vater für die Jugend, ein treuer Freund" in *Vision* 2000 (2/2011)

Soerens, Matthew and Hwang, Jenny., *Welcoming the Stranger: Justice, Compassion and Truth in the Immigration Debate*, Downers Grove: Illinois: IVP Books, 2009

Van Liere, Lucien M., "Fighting for Jesus on Ambon: Interpreting Religious Representation of Violent Conflict" in *Exchange* 40 (2011)

Volf, Miroslav., *Exclusion and Embrace*, Nashville, TN: Abingdon Press, 1996

Wallace, James A et al., *Lift Up Your Hearts: Homilies and Reflections for the B Cycle*, New York: Paulist Press, 2006

Weigel, George., *The End and the Beginning: John Paull II – The Victory of Freedom, the Last Years, the Legacy*, New York: Doubleday, 2010

Index of Names and Places

A
Abé xiv
Abu Dhabi 67
Abuja xiii
Afghanistan 66, 69, 94
Africa 125, 129, 148
African 111, 125, 138
Agostino Cassarolli 151, 156
Agostino Marchetto 84
Albert Nolan 56
Aldersbach 37
Algeria 110
Alitalia 107
Al Qaida 7, 104
Ambon xiv
Ambrosius 13
America 53, 55
Amsterdam 8
Anders Behring Breivik vii
Andrew Greeley 55, 65
Angelo Sodano 156
Arab world 110, 130
Ariel Sharon 48
Asia 129
Atocha
Augusto Pinochet 156
Australia ix, xv, 114, 122, 123, 164
Ayman al- Zahiri 7
Austria 63, 119

B
Baghdad 54
Bahrein 95
Barack Obama 12, 104, 154
Bavaria 37
BBC News 34, 104
Beijing 150
Belgium 147
Benedetto 12
Benedict XVI vii, xi, xiii, xv, xvii, xix, 4, 5, 8, 10, 12, 13, 41, 45, 46, 51, 52, 54, 56, 61, 62, 69, 78, 88, 89, 93, 103, 107, 122, 129, 134, 135, 147, 155
Benedictines 73, 123
Benghazi 10
Berlin 138
Bethlehem 4
Blaise Pascal 83
Bill Clinton 150
Birmingham viii
Bob Ellis ix
Bogota 78, 83
Bombay 71
Brazil xv, 155, 156
Bruno Volpe xvii
Byzantine 10
Bundestag 135

C

Cairo 114
Calcutta 121
Canada 114
Canterbury 136
Caspar von Silenen 101
Carmelengo 90
Chair of Peter 89
Chicago 134
Chile 156
China 94, 150, 151, 153
Christoph Schönborn 107, 120, 123
Christopher Hitchens xv
CIA (USA) 127
Circus Maximus 135
Clemens VII 41
Colonel Gaddafi 132
Colin Dueck 105
Columbia 78
Copenhagen 9
Cracow 45
Cuba 53

D

David F. Forte 5
Davos 115
Denver 132
Desert Storm 133
Diarmuid O' Murchu 145
Diaspora 133, 134
Diocletian 73
Diognetus 79
Dominus Iesus 5, 6
Dominique Mamberti xiii
Dubai 67

E

East Africa 23
East Europe 41, 63, 151
East Timor 54
Egypt xv, 113, 114
Ellen Wondra 6
England 104
Eugene III 90
Eurabia 63
European Union 103

F

Fatima 43, 44, 45, 51
Felici 41
Fodden 136
France 63, 84, 110, 111, 151
Francis George 134
Francis Stafford 132
Franz Beckenbauer 12
Frauenfeld 46
Frére Roger 121

G

G-8 109, 116, 117
Gemelli Clinic 44
George Gaenswein 47, 57
George W. Bush 66, 141
Genoa 115
Gerhard Lohfink 128

German 94, 132, 135, 141
Germany 6, 12, 63, 115, 119, 135, 151
Gerrado-Paul-Josef Cordes 120
Gleneagles 106
Great Britain 66, 136
Greece xv
Gulf war 69, 132

H
Hamas 153
Harold Camping 49
Heiligendam 115
Henry Kissinger 151
Hezbollah 153
Hilton 106
Hindu 69, 71
Holy See x

I
India 70
Indonesia xiv, 10
Innocent IV 91
Interpol 127
Iraq 55, 66, 141
Iran 141
Ishmael Noko 6
Islam xii, xiii
Israel 48, 71, 153
Italy ix, 63, 115

J
Jacques Chirac 110
Jean-Marie Le Pen 110
Jenny Hwang 139
John XXIII 67, 88
John Kennedy 48, 53
John l. Allen 4
John Onaiyekan xiii
John Paul II vii, xi, xix, 7, 12, 41, 42, 43, 44, 45, 47, 50, 52, 54, 55, 58, 61, 69, 71, 77, 78, 88, 103, 120, 121, 122, 147, 151, 155, 156, 157, 165
Jon Sobrino 117
Joseph Pierre 56
Joseph Ratzinger 1, 5, 8, 54
Joshua Mmali 104
Juan Maria Fernandez Krohn 45, 48
Julius II 102
Jyllands- Posten 9

K
Kampala 104
Karol Wojytla 42
Katrina Storm 49
Kenya 94, 139
KGB (Russia) 127
Kofi Annan 54
Kremlin 42
Kuwait 67, 111, 132

L

Lampedusa 112
Lateran 73, 87, 90, 136
Latin America 129, 148
Lebanon 10
Leonid Brezhnev 42
Libya 10, 132
Liverpool viii
London viii, 8, 9, 152, 156
Los Angeles 7, 59
Lucetta Scaraffia 47
Lucien Legrand 70, 71
Louvain-La-Neuve 147

M

Madrid xv, 8
Maghreb 8, 110
Mahatma Gandhi 53
Malcom Ranjith xvii
Maluku xvi
Manchester viii
Manuel Noriega 157, 158
Manuel II Paleogus 10
Martin Niemöller 5
Marseilles 111
Maryland 49
Matthäus Schiner 101
Mecca 136
Mehmet Ali Agca 41, 43, 47, 48, 52, 77
Michael Bray 49
Michael Corch x
Michael Root 6
Michelangelo 88, 101
Michelle 104
Middle East 109, 111
Mikhail Gorbachev 151
Milan 13
Miroslav Volf 147, 163
Mohammed Ali 2
Mohammed Bouazizi 112
Mohammed Bouyeri 8, 9
Montepellier 111
Montevideo 136, 137
Morocco 8, 110
Moscow 42
Mossad (Israel) 127
Mother Teresa 121
Movenpick 106
Mozambique 139
Mubarak 113, 114
Mumbai 71
Mussolini 136

N

Nathan Shcharansky 5
Nazi 43
New Orleans 49
Newt Gingrich 42
New York xv, 77, 84
Nicolas Sarkozy 85, 155
Nigeria vii, 16, 138
Nhat Hans 161
North Africa 115
North Korea 94, 141
Nostra aetate 5

O

Osama bin Laden 7, 104
Oscar Romero 3, 163
Oslo viii

P

Palatine Guard 100, 134
Palestine 4
Panama 157, 158
Pakistan 10
Panama 157, 158
Paris 132
Paul VI 93, 99, 106, 134
Paul Evaristo Arns 155
Pat Robertson 48
Pensacola 49
Persian Gulf 67
Peter Seewald xviii, 1, 3, 8, 11, 164
Peter von Hertenstein 101
Pius V 91
Pius IX 12, 54, 87
Poland 42
Portugal 45
Prussian war 136

R

Radio Vatican 94
Regensburg 10, 37
Richard Dawkins xv
Richard Nixon 151
Robert Mugabe 103
Roger Etchegaray 46
Roger Mahony 59
Roman Curia xix
Rudi Voller 12
Russia 132, 151

S

Sadam Hussein 69
Sao Paolo 155
Santa Cecilia 73
Samuel Huntington 69
San Salvador 118
Saudi Arabia 136
Seattle 115
Sedia gestatoria 77, 101
Sergio Vieira de Mello 53
Segolene Royal 85
Sidi Bouzid 112
Sistine Chapel 42, 88
Sheraton 106
South Korea 66
Soviet Union 42
Spain 8, 156
St. Peter's Basilica xi, 42, 45, 120
Stanislaw Dziwisz 44, 45
Stansted Airport 104
Syria 111
Sydney 122
Susan Maiolo 46, 52, 56, 57, 58
Swiss Guards 41, 47, 101, 102
Switzerland 46, 63, 97, 115

T

Taliban 66
Tahrir Square 114
Taize 121
Tanzania 14, 98, 139
Tertullian 12
Timothy Raddcliffe 106
Theo Van Gogh 8, 9
Theodosius 13
Tony Hendra 123
Tor Vergata 122
Trabazon 10
Tre Fontane 73
Tunisia 110, 111, 112, 115

U

Uganda 49, 104
UMISETA 14
United Kingdom xv, 104, 119, 151
United States 48, 49, 53, 94, 144, 151
UNO Headquarters 77
Utoya viii

V

Vatican ix
Vatican City x, 134, 136, 144
Vatican State x, 97, 140, 153
Vatileaks xviii
Vienna 107
Vietnam 132
Vilnius xiii

W

Washington 66, 152
William Boykin 142
William T. Cavanaugh 158
World War I 132, 141
World War II 130

Y

Yemen 111
Yoweri Museveni 104
Youcat 120

Z

Zurich 101